GAME FA

The Media Training Playbook
19 Cautionary Tales

BODINE WILLIAMS

Published by Q & A Books www.qandabooks.com

The information in this book is factual and complete to the best of the author's knowledge. The author and publisher disclaim any liability in connection with the use of this information.

Library of Congress Control Number: 2015930462

ISBN: 978-0-9908861-0-5

Interior design: Counterpunch Inc., Linda Gustafson

Printed in the United States of America
10 9 8 7 6 5 4 3 2 1

For Jean and Lionel

This book is also dedicated to Horace Greeley, who introduced the media interview and untold angst to subjects everywhere.

CONTENTS

INTRODUCTION

Most people are a lot smarter than they sound. And there's a reason for this. In school we were taught to focus on the written word, but in life it's what we say that matters—especially during interviews. In truth, you can't land a job or become president if you can't ace one.

Years ago, I sat in on a media training session in New York City. The client was the head of mergers and acquisitions for a Wall Street investment bank. He was handsome, clever, and as confident as one would wish. The coaching was intended to help him handle questions from business reporters and take analysts' calls with ease. It should have been a no-brainer. But about an hour into the session, after stumbling over some basic questions, he grew markedly less sure of himself. What had made the exercise so daunting?

As it turns out, my Wall Streeter isn't the only one with this problem. Over the years, I have learned that people don't lose their smarts during interviews—they lose themselves. That's because interviews are as much about what you know as how you present yourself. They reveal character, which is why they matter to hiring managers, voters, or reporters. In the heat of the moment, we forget what we should say or we reveal too much. Sometimes we even answer questions no one asked.

In public or behind closed doors, an interview can make or break a career. What subjects need are rules of conduct along with the tried-and-true media training techniques. That's what inspired me to write an illustrated guide for going on the record. I didn't want to tell people what to do—I wanted to show them how it's done.

In *Game Face: The Media Training Playbook, 19 Cautionary Tales,* you get to push the playback button on interviews as defining moments. Each chapter tells the story of a celebrated encounter: the players, the fallout, and the lessons learned. Most of the high-profile subjects assumed they knew what they were doing. You may smile or empathize, but you won't make the same mistakes. With the game face mind-set you will welcome the challenge.

Going "on the record" is an official response made in public or behind closed doors that is recorded for future reference or review.

"Defining moment" describes an unscripted interview moment that reveals character or affects the outcome of an event.

Game Face: the attitude of summoning your best self with the will to succeed.

Remember, Talk Is Autobiographical

It's relatively easy to present a false self when giving a speech or presentation. Punch lines can be written ahead of time and self-effacing laughter rehearsed. Verbal exchanges at interviews, hearings, and debates are different. They offer glimpses of the inner person. That's when the unconscious self serves up damaging revelations—often to questions not asked.

Even the celebrated wit Oscar Wilde underestimated the self-revelatory nature of talking back. Wilde, who joked he could spend hours on the placement of a comma when writing, neglected to show the same consideration when speaking at his trial. As Wilde's grandson, Merlin Holland, wrote in *The Real Trial of Oscar Wilde*, "One fatal witticism too many and Oscar had effectively talked himself into prison."

The Lord of Language

Oh, no, never in my life; he was a peculiarly plain boy.
—Oscar Wilde

John Sholto Douglas, the ninth Marquess of Queensberry, left a card with a hall porter at the Albemarle Club addressed "For Oscar Wilde posing Sodomite." The public insult was intended. Lord Queensberry wanted a swift end to Wilde's relationship with Lord Alfred "Bosie" Douglas, his twenty-year-old son.

When Wilde stopped at the club ten days later, on February 28, 1895, he received the card, which the porter had placed in an unsealed envelope. This was the final provocation. Queensberry had been hounding him for months and once turned up unannounced at Wilde's marital home. Still, it's impossible to fathom the motivation that led Wilde to pursue a private prosecution of Queensberry for libel.

It was an open secret that Wilde, the married father of two, and Bosie, the aspiring poet with the face of a sullen angel, had been inseparable since they met. The pair had even taken holidays together. Wilde knew of the terrible and enduring animosity between father and son. Queensberry was head of the most dysfunctional aristocratic household in London; two wives had bolted, his oldest son was said to have committed suicide, and he was on bad terms with his other sons. And dangerously, like Wilde, Queensberry craved public attention.

The Queensberry Rules, published in 1867, is a code of rules governing amateur boxing. It was so named because John Sholto Douglas, the ninth Marquess of Queensberry and a boxing promoter, publicly endorsed them. The code was actually written by John Graham Chambers.

Having been threatened by Lord Queensberry in the library of his own home, Oscar Wilde responded: "I don't know what the Queensberry rules are, but the Oscar Wilde rule is to shoot on sight."

On April 3, 1895, when Wilde arrived at the Old Bailey for the trial, he had two hit plays running in the West End: *The Importance of Being Earnest* and *An Ideal Husband.* He was the master of clever dialogue. Now Wilde was to star in a real-life Victorian drama.

The session began with questions from his lawyer, Sir Edward Clarke, who apparently was the only person in London who didn't know the truth about Oscar and Bosie. That would all change during Wilde's cross-examination by Edward Carson, the lawyer for Queensberry.

Oscar Wilde was indignant when asked about a love letter he wrote to Bosie. The fact that there were additional letters was volunteered by Wilde himself and introduced into evidence. Admittedly amusing to the spectators, it was more damning information. Wilde indulged and flattered himself on the stand. He chose to act as if the trial was about art and literature (matters on which he expounded most beautifully) and not about his immoral conduct as alleged by Queensberry.

Wilde was eloquent when defending the central themes in his famous book *The Picture of Dorian Gray.* "There is no such thing as a moral or immoral book," he insisted. "Books are either well written, or badly written."

Words! Mere words! How terrible they were! How clear, and vivid, and cruel! One could not escape from them.
—Oscar Wilde, *The Picture of Dorian Gray*, 1890

Edward Carson and Oscar Wilde were fellow students at Trinity College in Dublin. When Wilde was told that Carson had been retained by Queensberry, he reportedly said, "No doubt he will perform his task with the added bitterness of an old friend."
—Richard Ellmann, *Oscar Wilde*, 1987

CARSON: *The affection and the love that is pictured of the artist towards Dorian Gray in this book of yours might lead an ordinary individual to believe it had a sodomitical tendency, might it not?*
WILDE: *I have no knowledge of the ordinary individual.*
CARSON: *Oh, I see. But you do not prevent the ordinary individual from buying your book?*
WILDE: *I have never discouraged them. (Laughter.)*

The transcript sparkles with genius.

By now, Wilde knew he had made a terrible mistake bringing the case against Queensberry. Still, he couldn't resist the temptation to perform. All Carson had to do was keep him talking—Wilde served up a psychological cocktail of his best and worst self.

The defining moment came on the second day of the trial.

CARSON: *Did you ever kiss him? [Walter Grainger, an alleged lover]*

WILDE: *Oh, no, never in my life; he was a peculiarly plain boy.*

CARSON: *He was what?*

WILDE: *I said I thought him unfortunately—his appearance was so very unfortunately—very ugly—I mean—I pitied him for it.*

CARSON: *Very ugly?*

WILDE: *Yes.*

CARSON: *Do you say that in support of your statement that you never kissed him?*

Wilde tried to take back his words, but it was too late.

CARSON: *Why did you mention the boy's ugliness?*

WILDE: *I mention it because you sting me with the insolence of the question.*

CARSON: *Because I stung you by an insolent question?*

WILDE: *Yes, you sting me by an insolent question; you make me irritable.*

CARSON: *Did you say the boy was ugly, because I stung you by an insolent question?*

WILDE: *Pardon me, you sting me and insult me and try to unnerve me in every way. At times one says things flippantly when one ought to speak more seriously, I admit that I admit it—I cannot help it. That is what you are doing to me.*

In the morning of the third and final day, Wilde withdrew from the prosecution. The rent boys, private detectives, hotel clerks, chamber maids, and incriminating letters would not be needed by Queensberry's defense at this time. The marquess was not guilty of libel. And now the Crown had the evidence to try and convict Wilde for "gross indecency" under a law used to ban homosexual relationships.

Wilde's life was ruined.

The *Daily Telegraph* rushed with the news: "This man has now suffered the penalties of his career, and may well be allowed to pass from the platform of publicity which he loved to that limbo of disrepute and forgetfulness which is his due." The chorus of disapproval was soon a roar. Thanks to Wilde's gift for self-promotion, he was known simply as "Oscar," placing him in the pantheon of celebrities then and now. On this, the *Echo* had the last word: "Let him go in silence, and be heard from no more."

The scandal was so monstrous that Wilde's wife Constance was forced to leave the country with their small sons. They would never see their father again. Wilde served two years in jail and then went into exile in France, where he died at age forty-six.

All of this could have been avoided had Wilde, a Greek scholar, heeded Socrates' most famous dictum: "Know thyself." Whatever the stakes, interviews are a form of autobiography—only without an eraser.

If I could ask my grandfather a single question, it would have to be, "Why on earth did you do it?"
—Merlin Holland, *The Real Trial of Oscar Wilde*, 2003

Well, if you are my literary executor, you must be in possession of the only document *[De Profundis]* that gives any explanation of my extraordinary behavior with regard to Queensberry and Alfred Douglas. When you have read the letter, you will see the psychological explanation of a course of conduct that from the outside seems a combination of absolute idiocy with vulgar bravado.
—Oscar Wilde, letter to Robert Ross, April 1, 1897

Mastering Rule 1

Don't underestimate the self-revelatory nature of talking back. That's what makes trials, public hearings, and interviews so interesting; they reveal character. Listeners instinctively divide their attention between a speaker's words and his intention. The stress of public speaking can open a door to the subconscious. In his book, "The Psychopathology of Everyday Life," Sigmund Freud examines the psychological mechanisms behind mishaps in speech, including fatal answers.

The "Freudian slip" is named for Dr. Sigmund Freud (1856–1939), the founder of psychoanalysis, who is best known for his theories on the conscious and unconscious mind.

There is nothing wrong with showing emotion in an interview. You can show empathy, passion, disappointment, or contrition; any feeling is acceptable if it's sincere and doesn't distract from your message or the moment. Wilde's indignation was out of place. He had put himself on display, testing the bounds of tolerance. By doing so, the society he had scandalized claimed the greater indignation for itself.

Avoid any public display of bravado. Low key is best when difficulties mount. Acting out in denial is bound to make things worse. Distressed and embarrassed by the sudden loss of power and position, Wilde sought refuge in his natural gifts to captivate and amuse. He chatted as if he were dining in Belgravia rather than giving evidence at the Old Bailey. Wilde's refusal to accept the situation led to his inappropriate behavior. He reverted to type at the worst possible moment.

Donald Trump seemed to be acting on a similar impulse when, despite photographic evidence to the contrary, he forced his press secretary, Sean Spicer, to declare: "this was the largest audience to witness an inauguration, period." Trump also challenged the National Park Service's crowd estimates in an effort to refute media reports that Barack Obama had attracted more people to the Capitol for his first inauguration. Trump's combative stance and the public controversy consumed the first days of his presidency.

Never try to talk your way out of trouble. Under fire it's best to minimize and contain rather than expand and elaborate. To quote the authors of *The Elements of Style*, William Strunk, Jr., and E. B. White: "Do not overwrite. Do not overstate. Avoid the use of qualifiers. Do not explain too much. Avoid fancy words, be clear." Exchange "write" for "speak" and this reads like a critique of Wilde's trial performance.

Answer to the highest intention of the question. If you are asked a question intended to wound or embarrass you, but that has a basis in truth, hear the question as if it were being asked by a friend. It will help you to focus on the facts and not the threat. A tough question is just that, but you can neutralize the sting by calming your emotions before responding. An angry or testy reply always gives an advantage to the questioner.

Resist the temptation to live for and by publicity. The media thrive on triumphs and disasters with the same fevered intensity. Many have been heard to express dismay that the media turned against them, as if the media had ever been a friend.

There is no such thing as bad publicity, except for your own obituary.
—Dominic Behan, *My Brother Brendan*, 1965

Live by publicity, you'll probably die by publicity.
—Russell Baker, "Observer; Of Names, Zeal and Appetite," *New York Times*, December 3, 1986

Fame will go by and, so long, I've had you, fame. If it goes by, I've always known it was fickle.
—Marilyn Monroe, *Life*, August 17, 1962

Game Face Conduct

Never blame someone else for making you sound foolish. It's better to take ownership of offensive words than to appear dishonest. Besides, you'll look silly blaming your bad answers on the interviewer's questions. During the libel action, Oscar Wilde accused Edward Carson of trying to "insult" and "unnerve" him, but the prosecutor was only doing his job. *Your* words are *your* currency; it's up to you how well you guard or dispense them.

And Finally

Humor is subjective and should be attempted with caution. Jokes or one-liners about race, gender, sex, and religion are never appropriate. Oscar Wilde demonstrated, to his detriment, that jokes told at the expense of others impart feelings of intellectual or social superiority. Few people like a snob.

On the other hand, self-deprecating humor can be effective. In 1984, President Ronald Reagan was fighting the suggestion that, at seventy-three, he was too old to serve a second term. His imprecise responses in the first debate added to the speculation. When asked in the second debate if age was a factor, Reagan defused the issue and scored points with his quip: "I will not make age an issue in this campaign. I am not going to exploit, for political purposes, my opponent's youth and inexperience." Reagan even had Democratic rival Walter Mondale (age fifty-six) smiling.

By giving us the opinion of the uneducated, journalism keeps us in touch with the ignorance of the community.
—Oscar Wilde, Gilbert in "The Critic as Artist, Part 2," *Intentions*, May 1891

RULE 2

Know Your Story

An interview is an opportunity *if* you know your story. Henry Kissinger lost track of his narrative under the seductive gaze of Oriana Fallaci. The interview was to be a first-person account of the U.S. government's effort to end the Vietnam War. Instead, Kissinger took an imaginary ride to the Wild West, which ended badly. Back at the White House, President Richard Nixon was fuming. A chastened Kissinger learned the difference between an interview and a conversation.

A Lonesome Cowboy

I'll tell you. What do I care? The main point arises from the fact that I've always acted alone. Americans like that immensely. Americans like the cowboy who leads the wagon train by riding ahead alone on his horse. ... This amazing, romantic character suits me precisely because to be alone has always been part of my style.
—Henry Kissinger

In the fall of 1972, when talks to negotiate a peace agreement to end the Vietnam War were making headlines, the popularity of the National Security Advisor, Dr. Henry Kissinger, was so encompassing it seemed to diminish everyone around him—including the President of the United States, Richard Nixon.

The originator of "shuttle diplomacy," Kissinger was a master of mediation. He traveled the capitals of the world to broker deals and foster American interests. When he wasn't building strategic alliances in secret, he was courting Hollywood starlets in public. What made Kissinger's celebrity all the more intriguing was the fact that he rarely gave interviews. For one, he was a busy man who once boasted, "There can't be a crisis next week. My schedule is already full." But something compelled him to grant an interview to journalist Oriana Fallaci.

With flowing dark hair and an engaging Italian accent, Fallaci was an uncompromising journalist who had amassed

Why I agreed to it, I will never know.
—Henry Kissinger, Jack Anderson's syndicated column, May 17, 1979

her own share of influence, roving the globe and securing high-stakes interviews. She was known for a forceful charm and sharp disposition, which her mostly male subjects found disquieting. Kissinger, upon discovering that Fallaci had recently lent her ear to top North Vietnamese General Võ Nguyên Giáp, was drawn in. He agreed first to an off-the-record meeting, and then a formal interview.

Fallaci and Kissinger met on Saturday, November 4, 1972. They sat down in Kissinger's White House office, and at 10:30 a.m. Fallaci started recording. With her first question, she launched into Kissinger's dramatic announcement just days before that "peace was at hand." In actuality, negotiations for a cease-fire had taken a turn for the worse. The proposal put forth by the Communist government in the north had been rebuffed by the U.S.-backed government in the south, throwing the October 31 deadline into limbo. Fallaci was aware that behind the scenes the United States had stepped up its weapons delivery to Saigon, while the Communists were sending arms to Hanoi.

FALLACI: *[A]nd though you had confirmed that an agreement had been reached with the North Vietnamese, peace has not come. The war goes on as before, and worse than before.*
KISSINGER: *There will be peace. We have decided to have it and we will. It will come within a few weeks' time or even less; that is, immediately after the resumption of negotiations with the North Vietnamese for the final accord.*

The constant ringing of Kissinger's phone interrupted the flow. When it was President Nixon calling, Kissinger gave the Commander-in-Chief his full attention. Then he returned to Fallaci and the war. Kissinger resisted her suggestions that a

I did so largely out of vanity. She had interviewed leading personalities all over the world. Fame was sufficiently novel for me to be flattered by the company I would be keeping. I had not bothered to read her writings; her evisceration of other victims was thus unknown to me.
—Henry Kissinger, *Time*, October 8, 1979

grip on peace was tenuous and protested at least three times against any more questions on Vietnam. At one point, he pleaded, "Don't make me talk about Vietnam again please."

FALLACI: *But don't you find, Dr. Kissinger, that it's been a useless war?*

KISSINGER: *On this I can agree. But let's not forget that the reason why we entered into this war was to keep the South from being gobbled up by the North, it was to permit the South to remain the South. Of course I don't mean that this was our only objective. ... It was also something more ... But today I'm not in the position to judge whether the war in Vietnam has been just or not, whether our getting into it was useful or useless. But are we still talking about Vietnam?*

Sensing she could go no further, Fallaci changed tactics. Now Kissinger was really in trouble.

FALLACI: *Dr. Kissinger, how do you explain the incredible movie-star status you enjoy, how do you explain the fact that you're almost more famous and popular than a president? Have you a theory on this matter?*

KISSINGER: *Yes, but I won't tell you. Because it doesn't match most people's theories. ... My theory is completely different, but, I repeat, I won't tell you. ... Rather you tell me yours. I'm sure that you too have a theory about the reasons for my popularity.*

FALLACI: *I'm not sure, Dr. Kissinger. I'm looking for one through this interview. And I don't find it. I suppose at the root of everything there's your success. I mean, like a chess player, you've made two or three good moves. China, first of all. People like chess players who checkmate the king.*

Miss Fallaci is an ornament to her trade, and the text of the encounter should be required reading in all journalism courses. She ran the show from start to finish.
—Mary McGrory, *Washington Star-News*, November 26, 1972

KISSINGER: *Yes, China has been a very important element in the mechanics of my success. And yet that's not the main point. ... I'll tell you. What do I care? The main point arises from the fact that I've always acted alone. Americans like that immensely. Americans like the cowboy who leads the wagon train by riding ahead alone on his horse. ... All he needs is to be alone, to show others that he rides into the town and does everything by himself. This amazing romantic character suits me precisely because to be alone has always been part of my style.*

The Kissinger interview was published in its entirety in the *New Republic*. Portions were quoted in the Washington and New York dailies before landing in papers everywhere. First journalists criticized Kissinger's audacity, then came the ridicule. Columnist Mary McGrory told readers of *the Washington Star-News*, "If a middle-age Harvard professor who wears a vest and glasses, speaks with a German accent, has a double chin, a staff of 100, a chauffeured limousine wants to think of himself as a lonesome cowboy it's a free country, isn't it?" Political cartoonists depicted Kissinger as an overfed, big-hatted version of the iconic cowboy—a gauche Henry Fonda. President Nixon, meanwhile, was reportedly "white-lipped" with rage over his advisor's remarks. The Nixon-Kissinger relationship cooled overnight.

Kissinger protested that his words were taken out of context, but an indignant Fallaci threatened to make the tape recording public. It was too late for Kissinger to take a shot at telling his story.

Three days after the encounter, Nixon was reelected president in a landslide victory over Senator George McGovern. The Paris peace talks collapsed in December and the

At least a half dozen people who matter here in the White House hit the ceiling when they read that story. They called it the biggest ego trip anyone had ever taken.
—"Nixon and Kissinger: Triumph and Trial," *Time*, January 1, 1973

Always watch out, by the way, when a politician or star claims to have been "quoted out of context." A quotation is by definition an excerpt from context.
—Christopher Hitchens, "The Art of the Interview," *Vanity Fair*, December 2006

Vietnam War continued until the accord was finally signed on January 9, 1973. By then, Nixon had made Kissinger his secretary of state. In this new role, his notoriety grew to epic proportions, but for years Kissinger avoided the interview chair.

In the end, the two protagonists agreed on only one aspect of their now-famous encounter—a mutual resentment. To a *Time* magazine reporter, Fallaci insisted—somewhat disingenuously, given all the attention—that her interview with Kissinger was "one of the worst" she had ever had.

Fallaci put to rest all doubts when she published the full transcript of their conversation in her book, *Interview with History.* For his part, Kissinger described the interview as "the single most disastrous conversation I have ever had with any member of the press." And it was. Why? Interviews are guided conversations to the extent they are "conversations" at all. Kissinger didn't have a story to tell. He showed up and took questions, indulging himself as his vanities led him to blunder.

Then he declared that I had garbled his answers, distorted his thoughts, embroidered on his words, and he did so in such a clumsy way that I became angrier than Nixon and took the offensive.
—Oriana Fallaci, *Interview with History*, 1976

She described her interviews as "coitus" and "a seduction" and hated using interpreters ("the stranger's body between two people making love").
—Liz McGregor and John Hooper, "Obituary: Oriana Fallaci," *Guardian*, September 16, 2006

Mastering Rule 2

See the media interview as a business transaction. It's the exchange of knowledge or information for access to an audience for professional or personal advantage.

Know beforehand what you wish to achieve. Kissinger responded to questions, following where they led him. He didn't have a story to tell. Meanwhile, Fallaci had an agenda, the same one all reporters have—she wanted to make news.

The object of the exercise is what?
—Margaret Thatcher at the start of her interview with Terry Coleman, "You're Getting a Totally False Impression of Me," *Guardian*, November 2, 1971

Be prepared to answer questions with key messages. They should be clear, consistent, and advance a story line that sounds like a conversation. The best messages are positive: they tout results, especially those that benefit others. For example, Kissinger could have focused attention on the peace accord to frame the administration's foreign policy objectives and successes in Asia.

Practice using messages interchangeably to build a narrative. The skill requires you to be somewhat repetitive (as in consistent) without being redundant (as in overly scripted). This is not the same as "staying on message" regardless of the question asked. That's a shopworn maneuver that harms credibility. It also suggests the speaker lacks candor or is simply repeating words written by others.

Decide in advance what subjects are off limits. There could be any number of reasons for this: the information may be proprietary or otherwise confidential, the matter may be before the courts, or it may be too soon to talk about it. In Kissinger's case, an ill-advised comment could have impeded important negotiations. State the reason you are unable to discuss the matter. Do so with language you have pre-selected to avoid stumbling or appearing as though you are not prepared for the question.

Remember what the pundits say: *If you're explaining, you're losing.* Senator John Kerry's, "I was for the [Iraq] war before I voted against it" dogged the Democratic nominee for much of the 2004 U.S. presidential campaign. Explanations sound like distracting rationalizations after the fact. Besides, they remind the audience of past mistakes and waste time. Kissinger obviously erred in agreeing with Fallaci that Vietnam was a "useless" war. That led to a scene-stealing explanation of how the United States became ensnarled in Vietnam in the first place.

Expect to be asked the same question in different ways. This is a common practice of reporters and the nature of all inquiry. But when enough is enough, and after you have given your best response, say so. Rather than "Not Vietnam again," Kissinger should have said, "You have my answer. Can we move on?" The interviewer is unlikely to include your objection in the published piece. It's the journalist's job to test the limits. It's your job to set them.

Tactic

Find out all you can about the reporter's modus operandi and the news outlet in advance. It was obvious that neither Kissinger nor his staff did their homework before his interview. No one seems to have told him how Fallaci had earned her reputation. This was a woman who could call her book *Interview with History,* and did.

In his December 2006 homage to Fallaci in *Vanity Fair* magazine, Christopher Hitchens wrote: "Throughout the decades she scoured the globe, badgering the famous and the powerful and the self-important until they agreed to talk with her, and then reducing them to human scale."

Game Face Conduct

Before the interview, select the hat you'll be wearing (company spokesperson, parent representative, technical expert, and so on) and keep it on for the duration. Kissinger didn't appear to know if the interview was about him or his role as presidential advisor, which led to his indiscretions. Journalist Mary McGrory captured the psychological dynamic of the moment when she wrote, "She asked the question no man can resist: How come you're so wonderful?"

And Finally

Failure to identify a clear narrative going into the interview is the most common error subjects make. Without a map to guide them, many find themselves straying down roads best left untraveled. This happened to Howell Raines, the executive editor of the *New York Times,* who was at the helm when the *Times* racked up awards for its breathless coverage of September 11, 2001. At the time of his interview with Charlie Rose in 2003, Raines was in the media spotlight for his greatest failure. He had been fired after a plagiarism scandal rocked the paper and called attention to his management style.

Charlie Rose, a venue for thoughtful interviews, was the

Why an interview is *not* a conversation

Conversation is not an enterprise designed to yield an extrinsic profit ... it is an unrehearsed intellectual adventure. It is with conversation as with gambling, its significance lies neither in winning nor in losing, but in wagering.
—Michael Oakeshott, *The Voice of Poetry in the Conversation of Mankind,* 1959

From the direct sales pitch to a play for the goodwill of influential people, if it is designed to advance your career, it isn't conversation.
—Judith Martin, *Miss Manners' Guide to Excruciatingly Correct Behavior,* 2005

place for Raines to tell his story and remind people what it takes to win Pulitzer Prizes, which he had done as a managing editor and as a reporter. Instead Raines followed the line of questioning back into the controversy. He voiced criticism of the *Times'* publisher Arthur Sulzberger, Jr., and the news staff, complaining that they had "settled into a lethargic culture of complacency." As the *New York Observer* reported, "To many in the angered newsroom, the interview served as a moment of closure, a parting middle finger that summed up everything that had gone wrong within the paper since September 2001, and a reminder of why Mr. Raines could no longer be at the helm." Of the encounter, *Newsweek* declared: "His interview with Charlie Rose seemed to erase any residual sympathy for the hard-charging editor."

In this defining moment, Raines may have said too much and spoken too soon. It was hard to see how the interview had served his interest.

Consider the Audience

Linda Lay knew her story, but she forgot who she was speaking to when she appeared on NBC's *Today* show with her teary tale of woe. Perched on a sofa in one of her multi-million-dollar homes, Lay appeared to be claiming that she and her husband, the former Enron chairman Kenneth L. Lay, were on the verge of bankruptcy. Was she really looking for sympathy from the audience of hard-working men and women—most dashing off to work or returning home from the graveyard shift? Apparently so.

Down to Our Last Home

We are fighting for liquidity. We don't want to go bankrupt.
—Linda Lay

In the summer of 2001, financial troubles and rumors of fraud engulfed the Enron Corporation of Houston, Texas. Enron's plummeting stock price was eclipsing the claims coming from Enron executives that nothing was amiss. At the center of the campaign of denial stood Kenneth Lay, chairman of the energy-trading giant. When Jeff Skilling, the company's CEO, abruptly quit in August, Lay assured *BusinessWeek* that "there are absolutely no problems. The company is probably in the strongest and best shape that it has ever been in." And then in September, Lay told employees during an online chat that it was his "personal belief" that Enron stock was an "incredible bargain." That's what he was saying, but what Enron executives were doing, including Skilling and Lay, was dumping blocks of Enron shares.

Our liquidity is fine, as a matter of fact, it's better than fine. It's strong.
—Chairman Ken Lay, Enron webcast to employees, October 23, 2001

On October 22, Enron announced that the Securities and Exchange Commission had begun an "informal inquiry" into accounting practices with its partnerships. The next day, Lay answered questions from stock analysts, still insisting that the company was financially sound.

A few months later, Enron filed for Chapter 11 bankruptcy protection. Its collapse wiped out 5,000 jobs and $1 billion in retirement savings, making it the largest corporate failure in U.S. history. Twenty thousand former employees holding Enron stock faced staggering losses. In January 2002, the U.S. Department of Justice began a criminal probe. There was evidence that great crimes had been committed by "the smartest guys in the room," as later described in the 2003 bestselling book by that name.

The scandal precipitated a crisis for thousands of families, including Enron's first family—the Lays—who for decades enjoyed a fairy-tale life of privilege. On Saturday, January 28, 2002, Mrs. Lay welcomed a crew from NBC into her family's $2.8 million condo in Houston. The interview was a one-on-one exclusive with correspondent Lisa Myers, set to air on NBC's *Today* show in two segments. It would draw millions of viewers, among them former employees and shareholders financially crushed by Enron's fall.

This was Lay's chance to respond to the allegations and defend her husband's honor. She described Ken Lay, 60, as an "honest, decent, moral human being" who had been deceived by others. She wasted no time reaching out to touch her audience in a way no one expected. Linda Lay made the startling announcement that, like many others, she and her husband were in dire straits.

LAY: *Other than the home we live in, everything else is for sale. ... We are fighting for liquidity. We don't want to go bankrupt.*

MYERS: *According to published reports, your husband earned about $300 million in compensation and stock from Enron over the last four years. What happened to all that money?*

LAY: *By anyone's standards, it was a massive amount of money, and it's gone. It's gone. There's nothing left. Everything we had mostly was in Enron stock.*

Liquidity: a business term which refers to the ability of an asset to be converted into cash quickly and without any price discount.
—InvestorWords.com

Soon, the disgraced socialite was in tears as she described her husband's devastation when he learned that the company he founded was facing bankruptcy. Then Linda Lay shared details of the conversation that occurred a day before Enron's final collapse.

LAY: *He said he had tried everything he could think of and he could not stop it. ... We've lost everything but I don't feel Ken has betrayed me. I'm sad, I'm desperately sad but I don't know where to place my anger. I don't know who to get mad at. I just know my husband did not have any involvement.*

Few were moved by her claim of victimhood. Instead of bonding with her audience, Lay demonstrated just how out of touch she was with average Americans. How odd: she had been Ken Lay's secretary before they married and therefore should have been well acquainted with the vagaries of working life. Yet for this important interview, Lay came armed with messages for millionaires with her talk of properties (multiple) and "liquidity." Her misstep was an inspiration for late-night comics and editorial cartoonists.

"That's one weep-on-cue interview that backfired," wrote Robert Trigaux, a columnist for the *St. Petersburg Times*, as he summed up her public relations pitch. "Her hard to believe message?" he asked. "Husband Ken was as caught off guard by Enron's collapse as the company's 20,000-plus employees. Linda's second and more remarkable message during the *Today* interview? The Lays are in danger of personal bankruptcy."

In her syndicated column titled "Playing the Wife Card," economic writer Julianne Malveaux wondered if Lay equated her family's bankruptcy to the dire straits of Enron employees.

Her poor-mouthing earned a lashing from pundits who pointed out that, during the interview, she was wearing a wristwatch worth thousands. —Patrick Huguenin and Gina Salamone, "Ruth Madoff joins cursed wives club: Shame follows scammers' spouses," *New York Daily News*, Tuesday, June 30, 2009

"Bankruptcy law will protect the Lay house, allowing them to sell it and move into a smaller mansion," wrote Malveaux. "There is no protection for the people who lost their pensions with Enron."

After hearing from the disgraced socialite, reporters flocked to registry offices in several states to check on Ken and Linda Lay's real-estate holdings. As it turned out, the Lays owned about seventeen houses too many to convince anyone of her riches-to-rags story.

The *Wall Street Journal* confirmed that Ken and Linda Lay owned eighteen properties in Colorado and Texas and that only two were for sale. They also had a dozen vehicles, including three Mercedes and five Jeeps. In addition, the paper reported that Ken Lay still owned $17 million in non-Enron stock and other investments. *Mother Jones* magazine would later detail the elaborate insurance schemes the Lays used to shelter vast sums of money for their old age.

She caught the attention of *New York Times* columnist Frank Rich who remarked, "So Linda Lay takes us all for dupes, ready to be sold another bill of goods while she and her hubby plot their next escape for Aspen." Rich revealed that Lay's performance was coached by a "freelancing alum of Hill & Knowlton," a large PR firm that specialized in helping clients in crisis situations—often self-inflicted.

Though largely unchallenged, the interview was not a success, for Lay had opened herself to ridicule. *Time* magazine ran with a satirical piece entitled, "Is There Something Rotten in the Heart of Texas?" by Molly Ivins, who wrote, "Linda Lay's televised defense of her husband was a flop in Houston. For one thing, in Texas it's bad form to send the little woman out to fight your battles for you."

Editorial cartoonists depicted Linda and Ken Lay as latter-day Dickensian villains.

An illustration of "The New Homeless" features Ken Lay with a tin cup begging on a street corner accompanied by wife Linda, who carried a sign with the words —"Fighting for Liquidity," *Time*, February 11, 2002

Captioned, "The New Kind of Poverty," Ken Lay is seen standing on a podium under a spotlight speaking these words into a microphone: "I'm poor, my valet is poor, my chauffeur is poor, my chef is poor, my maid is ..." —*Newsweek*, November 22, 2003

Le secret des grandes
fortunes sans cause
apparente est un crime
oublié, parce qu' il a été
proprement fait.
[The secret of a great
fortune, for which there is
no apparent reason, is an
unknown crime that was well
executed.]
—Honoré de Balzac, *Le Père
Goriot*, 1835

Congress enacted the
Sarbanes-Oxley Act of 2002
(SOX) after the collapse
of Enron, WorldCom, and
other scandal-plagued
public companies. The key
provision requires Chief
Executive Officers and
Chief Financial Officers to
certify the representation
made in their companies'
regulatory filings.

Ken Lay gave no interviews and pled the Fifth at the Senate hearings in February 2002, reneging on a public pledge to tell what he knew about the crimes at Enron.

Four years later, he would be forced to answer questions in front of a judge, following the most extensive white-collar criminal investigation in the history of the F.B.I. In a true Honoré de Balzac moment, former Enron chiefs Ken Lay and Jeff Skilling went on trial in Houston on January 30, 2006. Together they faced thirty-six counts of fraud and conspiracy and up to two hundred years in jail. The prosecutor began by telling the jury that it was a simple case about "lies and choices." But there was nothing simple about the complex accounting scheme that was Enron.

On May 25, 2006, Lay was found guilty of ten counts of fraud and conspiracy. It was revealed during the trial that Lay had sold about $70 million in shares while encouraging shareholders to invest in the company, meanwhile never uttering a word about Enron's financial house of cards. Skilling was convicted of securities fraud, conspiracy, and insider trading and was sentenced to twenty-four years in prison.

Enron's accounting firm, Arthur Andersen LLP, was convicted of obstruction of justice for shredding documents relating to Enron's audits. The conviction was overturned on technical grounds, but the company, so tarnished by the scandal, ceased operations.

Weeks later on July 5, Lay died of a heart attack while vacationing in Aspen. His death, coming as it did before he was sentenced, erased his conviction and criminal record, rendering him an innocent man. This development would make it harder for employees and shareholders to recover money from Lay's $43.8 million-dollar estate. The chief beneficiary was his widow and champion.

Linda Lay knew what she wanted to say when she appeared on the *Today* show. However, she forgot to consider how her message would be heard. Playing the victim under the circumstances was bad enough, but she was discredited for insulting her audience.

Kenneth Lay, the deceased CEO of Enron Corp, defeated the Internal Revenue Service in the agency's bid to collect $3.9 million from his estate and his wife, the U.S. Tax Court ruled.
—Richard Rubin, "Kenneth Lay, Deceased Enron CEO, Wins Over IRS in Tax Court," *Bloomberg News*, August 30, 2011

Mastering Rule 3

The success of an interview depends on how the audience perceives the encounter. To select the right messages for audience members you have to know who they are. (What are their values, concerns, political loyalties, and so on.) To move people over to your side, start from where they are.

Don't expect the reporter to say if your message is good or bad. Reporters decide if you are newsworthy, but audiences decide if what you say is credible or not. To influence others, you have to speak their language. That calls for empathy which is the capacity to recognize and, to a meaningful degree, identify with the feelings and circumstances of others.

Consider what you bring to the audience. When you go out there with demands (sympathy, donations, votes, activism, respect, etc.), don't forget that audience members have expectations of their own (candor, honesty, insight, reassurance, etc.). In this case, Linda Lay was asking for support while offering nothing in return. And by turning the spotlight on herself, she highlighted just how much wealth and privilege was generated by Enron insiders.

Avoid melodrama. Television is a "cool medium," so said 1960s communication guru Marshall McLuhan. Treat the television camera as a person in the room. Therefore you don't need to play up to the camera or amplify yourself. If you do, you will appear fake or overwrought to viewers.

Don't assume the experts know best. While it's a good idea to seek professional advice, never suspend your own judgment—or common sense. Linda Lay, a multimillionaire, was counseled by a public relations veteran to voice a storyline that was, basically, "I've got financial trouble, too." It was a disastrous strategy, which led to a disastrous performance and ensuing ridicule.

Don't count on surrogates to demonstrate superior judgment when speaking on your behalf. In 2001, Raoul L. Felder, the lawyer who represented New York Mayor Rudy Giuliani during his bitter divorce from Donna Hanover, set eyes skyward when he announced to a curbside gathering of scribes the following: "The marriage is dead; it's awaiting interment. Mrs. Giuliani is just refusing to show up for the funeral." Earlier inside the courtroom, Felder was just as dramatic, saying, "The leitmotif here is Donna Hanover—that isn't even her maiden name, by the way, that's the name of her former husband—will have to be dragged from the chain of the chandeliers in Gracie Mansion by the next mayor, whoever that will be." Mayor Giuliani had no comment on his spokesman's comments.

Game Face Conduct

Never underestimate your audience. It's always a mistake. Linda Lay could have used the valuable air time on the *Today* show differently. She might have expressed her regret for all the lost jobs, pensions, and broken promises. Or she could have defended her husband without the crocodile tears. Few could blame Lay for Enron's collapse, but most who saw the interview found fault with her callous and condescending attempt to gain sympathy.

And Finally

Messages don't discriminate. In fact, they don't care where they wind up. While they should be targeted to specific audiences, they can and will be heard anywhere. Henry "Hank" Paulson was the chief executive officer and chairman of the financial services firm Goldman Sachs Group. While attending an investment conference on January 28, 2003, Paulson was asked about the possibility of a second round of layoffs. To shareholders, he came off sounding like a man who was keeping his options open: "I don't want to sound heartless, but in almost every one of our businesses, there are 15 or 20 percent of the people that really add 80 percent of the value. I think we can cut a fair amount and not get into the muscle and still be well positioned for the upturn."

Heartless was how Paulson sounded to his twenty thousand employees. The investment bankers, analysts, and secretaries who worked at Goldman Sachs might also have added the word "disloyal" to describe their boss's remarks. A swift apology was needed and it arrived in the form of a voice mail to each employee the following Monday morning. Paulson apologized for his "glib and insensitive response," saying he was profoundly embarrassed about his "choice of words" that were "completely at odds with my respect for the people we have had to let go." In this case, a message intended for an external audience landed with a thud at Paulson's front door.

Don't Presume You'll Rise to the Occasion

Soldiers are not sent into battle in the hope that they will "wing it" or "rise to the occasion." They perform at the highest level of training. The same goes for media interviews. Don't count on your past accomplishments or a flash of verbal inspiration to get you through. On the spot, you are more likely to freeze or overreact. That's what happened to Alexander Haig, the former supreme commander of NATO and U.S. secretary of state. Haig made a disastrous appearance before the White House press corps, and he did it on the day the whole world was watching.

The Day Reagan Was Shot

As of now, I am in control here.
—Alexander Haig, Jr.

On March 30, 1981, John Hinckley tried to assassinate President Ronald Reagan as he was leaving the Washington Hilton Hotel. Hinckley fired six bullets in nine seconds. The first bullet hit White House Press Secretary James Brady in the head. Thomas K. Delahanty, a police officer, and Timothy J. McCarthy, a Secret Service agent were also wounded. McCarthy extended his body to shield "the target"— exactly as he was trained to do. He took a bullet for the president and was a hero before the day was over.

When I look at that video, it surprises me too that I turned around and assumed the position I did. I'll take credit for it, of course, but it was really based on training. —Timothy McCarthy, CBS News, 2006

However, a stray bullet ricocheted off the limousine and into the president's chest as he was pushed onto the seat. Reagan walked into the hospital but collapsed in the emergency room. As news of the shooting circled the globe, members of Reagan's cabinet began gathering in the White House to manage the crisis. It had only been 70 days since they were sworn in. They positioned themselves in the Situation Room, located in the basement of the West Wing. The group included Secretary of State Alexander Haig, Defense Secretary Caspar Weinberger, Treasury Secretary Donald T. Regan, and Richard Allen, the national security advisor. Allen thought to bring along his personal tape recorder.

They began briefing congressional and world leaders. Chief of Staff James A. Baker III was sending medical updates from the president's bedside. Vice President George H.W. Bush was in an airplane over Texas. In the tense and hurried atmosphere, the men were engaged in petty power struggles while dealing with questions about possible Soviet threats and military alerts. This was, after all, the Cold War—a time when the Soviet Union was armed with massive nuclear weaponry, most of it pointed at targets in the United States.

Upstairs in the pressroom, reporters were peppering Deputy Press Secretary Larry Speakes with questions. They were demanding to know who was in charge while the president was incapacitated.

REPORTER: *Who's running the government now?*

REPORTER: *If the president goes into surgery and goes under anesthesia, would Vice President Bush become the acting president at that moment or under what circumstances does he?*

SPEAKES: *I cannot answer that question at this time.*

REPORTER: *Larry, who'll be determining the status of the president and whether the vice president should, in fact, become acting president?*

SPEAKES: *I don't know the details on that.*

Haig overheard this exchange while glancing at the TV monitors in the communication center next to the Situation Room. Alarmed by what he heard being broadcast live to friend and foe, Haig rushed upstairs through a maze of corridors into the pressroom. He lunged toward the open microphones.

He was about to make matters worse.

REPORTER: *Who is making the decisions for the government right now? Who's making the decisions?*

Joseph Tumulty, Woodrow Wilson's private secretary from 1913 to 1921, was effectively the first press secretary. His role was intended to limit access to the president. Today, the White House press secretary is a key presidential appointment.

"Be Prepared" is the motto of the Boy Scouts, coined by Sir Robert Baden-Powell, who founded the movement in 1908. When "BP," as he was known, was asked by a British reporter what scouts should be prepared for, he replied: "Any old thing."

HAIG: *Constitutionally, gentlemen, you have the president, the vice president, the secretary of state, in that order, and should the president decide he wants to transfer the helm to the vice president, he will do so. As of now, I am in control here, in the White House, pending the return of the vice president and in close touch with him. If something came up I would check with him of course.*

The moment would become an unshakable part of the biography for the four-star general, who had served as chief of staff during the final days of the Nixon presidency.

Unfortunately, Haig got his facts wrong. Under the U.S. Constitution, the vice president, the speaker of the house, and the president pro tem of the Senate—three people—come before the secretary of state in order of succession. And the secretary of defense becomes the military commander (after the president) of the armed forces.

Haig's misstep was immediately apparent according to transcripts of the Situation Room tapes, released in 2001. In them, Defense Secretary Weinberger, who had no idea Haig had gone to the pressroom, scolds the secretary of state on his return: "Well, I think we could have done a little better if we had concentrated on a specific statement to be handed out. When you're up there with questions, why then it's not anything you can control." Weinberger was correct in his assessment. Still it was Haig who took action. He understood that in a crisis what you say can be as important as what you do. The reporters needed information. However, Haig was anything but reassuring. His comments made him a distracting and controversial element in an already unsettling moment.

Haig learned a painful lesson that day: even in an

emergency, the media showed no mercy. He was sharply criticized by journalists across the country as the crisis was unfolding. Speakes' lackluster performance was ignored or discounted. More was expected of Haig, but the good soldier was not prepared.

Four hours after the shooting, Vice President Bush returned to Washington and the Situation Room was closed down. The president was out of surgery; the worst was over. Two days later, on April 1, the *New York Times* suggested that Haig had "appeared tense" using "tough-sounding language." On April 3, William Safire wrote, "He was sweating, straining to keep calm, a man apparently on the edge of panic." The *Washington Post's* Martin Schram described Haig's misstatement as "a shaky, emotional claim over national television of a constitutional authority in the line of presidential succession." The criticism went on for weeks.

Haig would devote an entire chapter—more than seventeen thousand words—in his 1984 autobiography, *Caveat: Realism, Reagan, and Foreign Policy*, to explain the eight words he spoke on that historic day.

"My appearance became a celebrated media happening. Edited versions were played and replayed many times. Even if I wished to do so, it is now too late to correct the impressions made. ... Perhaps the camera and microphone magnified the effects of my sprint up the stairs. ... Certainly, I was guilty of a poor choice of words, and optimistic if I imagined that I would be forgiven the impreciseness out of respect for the tragedy of the occasion. My remark that I was 'in control pending the return of the vice president' was a statement of fact that I was the senior cabinet officer present. ... Less precise, though in the same context, was my statement that 'constitutionally' [...]. I ought to have said 'traditionally' or

Q: To what do you attribute your success?
OLIVIER: The confidence to perform and the humility to prepare.
—Laurence Olivier, on the occasion of his knighthood, 1947

'administratively' instead of constitutionally." (Note Haig's editing of his actual words. He omitted "here, in the White House," which sounded to his critics like a grab for presidential power.)

Seventeen years later, in 2001, when asked by CBS News what he thought of his "famous pronouncement," Haig said, "I don't worry about midgets. ... Only the beltway gang care a hoot about it. The rest of the world, as I told you, was assured."

Whatever Haig's public pronouncements, his misstep on that fateful day was cause for private regret. His press briefing is almost as memorable as the attempted assassination of the president. Haig made assumptions about his abilities. He spoke in haste and never lived it down.

Alexander Haig died on February 20, 2010. In obituaries and tributes, as predicted, Haig's misstep in the aftermath of the assassination attempt was remembered as the defining moment of his career.

He knew that the third paragraph of his obit would detail his conduct in the hours after President Reagan was shot.
—Lyn Nofziger, *New York Times*, February 20, 2010

He never lived down his televised response to the 1981 assassination attempt on President Ronald Reagan. Some saw the comment as an inappropriate power grab.
—Associated Press, February 20, 2010

Mastering Rule 4

An interview is an opportunity *if* you're prepared. Take a minute to create a headline (the most important thing you want people to remember), or one will be created for you.

Know your intentions before you step into the spotlight. Consider whether your goal is to inform, reassure, motivate, explain, or inspire. If you don't know, your audience won't either. Haig's problem was that he had two primary objectives: He wanted to warn the Russians and he wanted to assure Americans. He was conflicted, and so was his communication.

Don't confuse your area of expertise with the skills needed to answers questions from reporters. There are times when it's imprudent to take questions. You do not want to be "thinking on your feet" in a room full of reporters or any audience. (Haig should have exited after reading a statement prepared in advance. It was exceedingly poor judgment to invite questions given the crisis and the frenzied atmosphere in the pressroom.) Avoid or delay questions until you have the facts to respond effectively. In the meantime, a statement will do. Statements leave little room for misinterpretation or speculation and they are rarely misquoted.

L'esprit d'escalier, or "wit of the staircase," is a French expression that captures the irony of knowing what to say only after the moment has passed and you are departing.

Answer the question you're asked, not the question you fear. Sometimes subjects over-anticipate the level of response required. The answer to "Who's making the decisions?" should have been, "The vice president acts for the president." Talk of the Constitution and "transferring the helm" was scary, unnecessary, and introduced by Haig himself. Haig was well aware of just how vulnerable the young administration was and his shaky presentation betrayed worry (and his own ambition).

Critical situations call for economy of language. The more you say, the less control you have over your message or what's being heard. Don't leave it to your audience to edit and interpret your various points to determine what's most important. If you do, assume they will get it wrong.

Remember, you communicate through style, tone, and intention as well as with words. The audience takes in everything about the speaker in a matter of seconds. If you appear agitated or tense, that's how you will "sound" regardless of what you say. Psychologist Albert Mehrabian's studies of nonverbal behavior suggest that the weight people give to face-to-face encounters is 7 percent to the actual words spoken, 38 percent to vocal inflection, and 55 percent to facial expression.

Don't leave reporters out of the loop in a crisis. Be sure to provide constant updates, even if you are merely repeating what is already known. Like nature, reporters abhor a vacuum. But once you have the full picture, get all the bad news out at once. If you delay, you risk the drip-drip-drip of negative coverage in the days to come.

Le style c'est l'homme même. [The style is the man himself.]
—Georges-Louis Leclerc, Comte de Buffon, from his inaugural speech at the French Academy, August 25, 1753

One cannot communicate a word; the whole person, the whole man always comes with it.
—Peter F. Drucker, *Management: Tasks, Responsibilities, Practices,* 1974

It's not just the words you choose to send to the other person that make up the message. ... The words themselves are meaningless unless the rest of you is in synchronization.
—Roger Ailes, *You Are the Message: Getting What You Want by Being Who You Are,* 1988

Tactic

When asked multiple questions at once, as often happens at press conferences, do not attempt to recapture the questions or the sequence, or to answer them all. (For example: "First, let me respond to question three and then return to the other two.") Cherry-pick the question that is closest to your key message, and let the event unfold. If the reporter wants to return to a question (which almost never happens), he will.

Game Face Conduct

Never miss an opportunity to show your humility. It's the trademark of a truly accomplished person. The media traffics in reputations—inflating and deflating them at will. With President Reagan and agent McCarthy cast as heroes, the role of public villain fell to Haig. He had drawn attention to himself at a time when all the president's men were expected to stand together. In his own assessment of the event, Haig ignored the possibility that his well-earned confidence may have given way to overconfidence.

Brutus: ... as he was valiant, I honor him. But, as he was ambitious, I slew him.
—William Shakespeare, *Julius Caesar*, Act 3, Scene 2

And Finally

Any time there is a live camera in the room, the most important conversation you are having is with the television audience at home. And it's likely to be a much bigger crowd. If you are the speaker, it's important to remember that the broadcast audience does not have the context of what's actually taking place in the room. Howard Dean, the former governor of Vermont, learned that painful lesson. On January 19, 2004, after a third-place finish at the Iowa Democratic caucuses, an oddly upbeat Dean was rallying his supporters. With a hoarse voice and a poor microphone system, Dean's rebel yell sounded hysterically shrill. It left a surreal impression on the viewers at home. The people in the room thought nothing of it, but the media wouldn't let it go. According to *The Hotline*, the Dean scream aired 633 times on cable and broadcast news within a few weeks. The "Dean Scream" or the "I Have a Scream" speech was even parodied on *Saturday Night Live*. Arguably, this media moment hastened the end of Dean's run for president.

Don't Overreach in Your Speech

Don't try to outsmart your audience. You might lose more than you gain. Before the Internet bubble burst, CBS's *60 Minutes* came calling at the offices of Razorfish to interview Jeffrey Dachis and Craig Kanarick, co-founders of the new web design and consulting company. In two short years, the pair had become legends in Silicon Alley, a few cyber-blocks of Manhattan. When asked the reason for their success, Dachis offered up fancy words and plenty of jargon.

The Slipper Room

We've asked our clients to recontextualize their business.
We've recontextualized what it is to be a business service.
—Jeffrey Dachis

At the dawn of the millennium, American companies were bombarded with news about the potential of the Internet and how it could help boost sales. Business to business technology had become the "new big thing." In hailing the virtues of a digital world, industry analysts conjured up images of an epic battle. It was the new economy versus the old economy, with those who get it versus those who don't. Fueled by the fear of being left behind, just about everyone jumped on the bandwagon looking for ways to do business on the Web.

California reigned as the leader for Web development, but New York—home to Razorfish Inc.—was experiencing a burgeoning of Internet businesses. Downtown had become a place brimming with "smart, young artistic types who 'got' the Net," as described by *BusinessWeek*. Razorfish was founded in 1995 by childhood friends Jeffrey Dachis and Craig Kanarick. Their consultancy delivered Web-based advertising and design services to businesses delving into e-commerce.

Our business is infested with idiots who try to impress by using pretentious jargon.
—David Ogilvy, author of *Confessions of an Advertising Man*, 1963

Dachis, the chief executive officer, was "the business guy" who had traveled an unusual route to the executive suite. He earned his master's in Performing Arts Administration;

then he tried his hand as a dancer, model, disc jockey, and founder of a small promotional company called In Your Face. Kanarick, "the design guy," had attended MIT's Media Lab and later moved to New York, where he freelanced for a digital magazine and taught at New York University. In 1994, their paths crossed and months later they met in Dachis' East Village apartment, where Razorfish was born. It would go from Web design to Web supremacy in a dot-com minute.

Advertising giant Omnicom Group bought a stake in Razorfish and provided Dachis and Kanarick with offices in SoHo. The duo got lucky with a series of contracts that boosted Razorfish's sales from $300,000 in 1995 to $3.6 million in 1997. Soon the company was attracting big, brand-name clients.

Razorfish embarked on a series of bold moves, acquiring a host of smaller, European digital-consulting firms in 1998 and launching its IPO on the NASDAQ a year later. The company had quadrupled revenues and increased its workforce. Once seen as a Web graphics and advertising agency, Razorfish now rejected this classification. The company stated that its primary business was to help clients "establish a brand in an expanding digital world."

With success came the media attention Dachis and Kanarick craved. It was reported that an employee was a "fish" who received constant reminders to "be the brand"— Razorfish language for being creative and cutting edge. One *BusinessWeek* writer called this new school of management a throwback to drinking the Kool-Aid, Ken Kesey–style. This cliquish mind-set ran 24/7. Dachis and Kanarick became part owners of The Slipper Room, an intimate Lower East Side lounge for the arts and technology types. The

In 1997, Internet investments totaled $1.88 billion, a 1,300 percent increase from Internet-related funding two years prior.
—Price-Waterhouse, April 8, 1998

Indeed, Dachis was something of a Ken Kesey for the Net generation. Kesey, the hippie novelist who came to fame in the 1960s, drove around the country with his band of Merry Pranksters in a bus painted with psychedelic designs. He served up LSD-laced Kool-Aid and declared that people were "on the bus" or "off the bus" depending on whether they drank it.
—Heather Green, *BusinessWeek*, March 19, 2001

Slipper Room hosted theme parties and burlesque shows all complemented by high-priced, personally branded martinis, the Dachismo and the Craigar.

Profiles about the founders noted their excesses, which ironically included their flaunting of old-guard status symbols such as Prada suits, a Corvette convertible, and a Harley-Davidson motorcycle. Articles mentioned how Dachis couldn't resist bringing his beloved Weimaraner, Sophie, into the workplace and how business was shut down so that 1,200 employees could enjoy a three-day party in Las Vegas; another time it was three days of white-water rafting in Oregon.

Dachis talked the brand as he lived it. With CNET he said, "Who is going to be up there with Razorfish? ... I'll argue we're six or seven generations ahead of any of our competitors." Reporters cringed at the cockiness. Speaking to the *New York Times* about the flood of Internet IPOs, Dachis remarked, "I don't want to be lumped in with the hucksters of the world, because we have the real deal. ... I'm sorry, but there are sheep and there are shepherds, and I fancy myself to be the latter."

The buzz on Razorfish grew so loud it attracted *60 Minutes*, the CBS news-magazine program and originator of the high-stakes interview. By now Dachis and Kanarick, both thirty-three years old, were each worth about $250 million. For their big on-camera moment, the Web duo received the television crew in their sixteen-thousand-square-foot office. Dachis sported a sleek black suit, black tie, and spiky hair while Kanarick wore a flashy purple suit and yellow shirt. In contrast, the silver-haired reporter Bob Simon was inconspicuous in his earth-tone suit. His questions, however, would be cutting edge.

Hyperbole: a way of speaking or writing that makes someone or something much bigger, better, smaller, worse, more unusual, etc., than they are.
—*Cambridge Advanced Learner's Dictionary*, 3rd Edition

On February 15, 2000, the *60 Minutes* clock began its ominous countdown. Seconds later, TV viewers heard Simon's soothing voice: *"The nexus of all this energy is called Silicon Alley, a group of old sweatshops in lower Manhattan. Kanarick and his partner, Jeff Dachis, started Razorfish there. The company is now worth $4 billion and is one of the most successful companies on the Web."*

SIMON: *Successful at what?*
DACHIS: *Good question. We've asked our clients to recontextualize their business. We've recontextualized what it is to be a business service ... and that'll continually ...*
SIMON: *You know, there are people out there, such as myself, who have trouble with the word, "recontextualize." Tell me what you do, in English.*
DACHIS: *We provide services to companies to help them win.*
SIMON: *So do trucking firms. What is it you do?*
DACHIS: *Our talent is to do a certain thing, whereas the trucking firm ...*
SIMON: *Yes, but what is it you do?*
DACHIS: *We radically transform businesses to invent and reinvent them.*
SIMON: *That's still very vague.*

After a pregnant pause, Kanarick stepped in and offered: "Business strategy."

The duo, used to overreaching with their tech talk, had been yanked back to earth. A seasoned interviewer, Bob Simon knew a defining moment when he heard one. According to Warren St. John of *Wired* magazine, Simon at that moment looked "as if he might high-five his cameraman."

Robert Birge of the Boston Consulting Group felt the virtual TKO punch sent throughout the Internet world. "It was a very strange moment," said Birge. "To see those two guys on national TV not making sense made you realize it wasn't just you who didn't get it." Jason Calacanis, an editor with the *Silicon Alley Reporter* and an acquaintance of Dachis and Kanarick, observed, "It was the first time anyone had ever made them look stupid."

After the *60 Minutes* debacle, it was still business as usual for Razorfish. But the sun was setting on Internet companies and Razorfish soon found itself in the shade. Rumors swirled about its internal problems, chiefly personality conflicts. Company shares dropped. Investors worried. The company joined a line up of Internet businesses issuing a litany of bad-news reports, indications of impending troubles. Razorfish moved to cut costs, shedding employees the old-fashioned way—with layoffs.

Businesses meanwhile turned to the established brands that were now sharpening their skills in e-commerce. Upstarts with their Internet-laden jargon suddenly seemed less awe inspiring. The tech bubble of hyper-confidence, hyper-projections, and hyper-buying had simply burst. Razorfish's stock price plummeted from a high of $57 a share the previous year to a low of $1.

A subdued Dachis commented on lessons learned, telling *BusinessWeek*, "Somehow what we did got misinterpreted. So we have to go out of our way to be humbler." As he spoke, Razorfish continued to hemorrhage capital, clients, and key employees. Its inability to cash in on the *60 Minutes* opportunity certainly didn't help. In May 2001, Dachis and Kanarick resigned from the company they founded.

In reporting on their departure, T.C. Doyle of *VARBusiness* magazine revisited the Web guys' verbal fumble on *60 Minutes*. "Dachis, for example, grew to epitomize the false prophets that the new economy seemed to produce in great numbers," wrote Doyle. "After he told CBS's *60 Minutes* that Razorfish's principal business was 'recontextualizing' organizations, he became a lightning rod of ridicule that continues to this day."

Razorfish endured under new management, but eventually lost its independence when it was bought by a private consulting group in 2002. It was sold, and then bought again several times. Years later, Dachis would reflect on what he considered the end of an era: "It was the last day of Silicon Alley. ... When Craig and I stopped going to work on May 5, [2001], there wasn't really a Silicon Alley anymore."

Volumes would be written on the dot-com era of hyped-up share prices and paper billionaires, but it was also the overblown rhetoric that had fueled the ride. The *60 Minutes* interview was a painful reminder for the pair that when speaking on the record, low tech is best.

I've looked up "recontextualize" a million times in a million places and it's just not a real word. So that's the first problem. The second problem is that [Bob] Simon gave them several kicks at the can. Now, I don't know about you, but none of my potential customers would give me all of those chances, and say, "I still don't understand."
—Andy Craig, "You Know What Your Company Does. Can You Explain It in 30 Seconds?," Alison Stein Wellner, *Inc.*, 2007

Mastering Rule 5

Avoid words that draw attention to themselves. Words that invite close inspection obscure context and detract from your messages.

Don't exaggerate if your goal is to be taken seriously. You may grab attention by hyping the facts, but you'll weaken your hand in the long run. In June 2013, Edward Snowden, a contractor for the United States National Security Agency, leaked details of the U.S. government's classified surveillance programs. Soon in interviews, Snowden began describing U.S. government agencies as "adversaries," their programs as "architecture of oppression," and predicted a future of "turnkey tyranny." By indulging in hyperbole, Snowden set the wrong tone which made it more difficult for him to shape public debate on the important issues around the individual's right to privacy.

Avoid using "loaded language." These words go beyond buzzwords and jargon because they appeal to emotion over reason and polarize audiences. Words such as terrorist, socialist, racist, sexist, and so on should not be trivialized or exploited. *Washington Post* columnist Michael Gerson takes aim at one word that often tops the list, writing, "Nazism is not a useful symbol for everything that makes us angry, from Iraq to abortion. It is a historical movement, unique in the ambitions of its cruelty."

On NBC's *Today* show in 1998, Hillary Clinton uttered the words "vast right-wing conspiracy," referring to those attempting to impeach her husband, Bill Clinton. She was mocked by conservative pundits. Clinton would later say, "Looking back, I see that I might have phrased my point more artfully."

When Clinton appeared before the House Select Committee on Benghazi, she left the loaded language to others.

Clinton's disciplined performance, command of facts and pure stamina may bear out her calculation that a public performance would work to her benefit, as well as remind her opponents why she is an imposing candidate. —Anne Gearan, Karen Tumulty and Elise Viebeck, *Washington Post*, October 22, 2015

Don't answer questions with slogans. The phrase "helping people win" is not a message. Messages differentiate people, products, and services and they are factual. As the *60 Minutes* interviewer noted, there are no companies that are in the business of helping clients lose.

Remember—unlike slogans, messages have to deliver. Advertising jingles are catchy and fun but they don't have to mean anything. For example, Coke's "The real thing" is a slogan that could apply to a hammer. "Coca-Cola is the best-selling soft drink in history,"—now that's a message. Advil's slogan, "We are stronger than pain," would sound strange if repeated by the company's CEO in response to a question because it's not a message. He's more likely to say, "For 25 years, millions of people have trusted Advil to relieve their aches and pains."

Avoid trying to sound profound or fanciful. A lot has been written about President George W. Bush's gaffes and malapropisms. However, the most interesting of Bush's verbal eccentricities was his tendency to overreach when responding to questions. When overreaching, the speaker speaks for dramatic effect rather than for clarity. In June 2001, after their first meeting, Bush and Russian President Vladimir Putin held a joint press conference. To the question "Is [Putin] a man Americans can trust?" Bush responded, "I looked the man in the eye. I found him to be very straightforward and trustworthy. We had a very good dialogue. I was able to get a sense of his soul." Some were bemused by Bush's attempt to sound deep; others, like Republican Senator Jesse Helms, were alarmed at the president's blue-sky assessment of the former KGB operative. "Soul mates" or "soul brothers" was

Message vs. Slogan

Message: a communication containing a point or theme that defines or differentiates.
Slogan: catchphrase or tag line used in advertising.

The Slogan

[a] Does she...or doesn't she?
[b] A mind is a terrible thing to waste
[c] A Diamond is Forever
[d] It takes a licking and keeps on ticking
[e] Reach out and touch someone
[f] Just Do It.
[g] Where's the beef?
[h] Don't leave home without it
[i] Breakfast of Champions

The Company

[a] Clairol
[b] United Negro College Fund
[c] De Beers
[d] Timex
[e] AT&T
[f] Nike
[g] Wendy's
[h] American Express
[i] Wheaties

how the media headlined stories critical of Russia's backward slide under Putin. However, the best line belonged to Senator John McCain, who quipped, "I looked into Putin's eyes and I saw three letters, a K, a G, and a B." President Bush's tendency to lofty speech was perhaps to counter comments about his verbal IQ. In overreaching, Bush left himself open to charges of naiveté.

Tactic

If you have it, flaunt it. In media training parlance, this is called "flagging." You flag something with language that gets people to sit up and pay attention. This is the moment when the reporter pauses with his or her pen in midair. When flagging, you are telling the audience that what you are about to say is important. Use words like "What's exciting about this ... " or "In two years ... " or "Look for ... " and so on. You flag something you're proud of—but it has to be real. Knowing when and how to flag is important. Too much flagging is a flag in itself.

Game Face Conduct

Avoid appearing boastful. Dachis' comment, "I'll argue that we are six or seven generations ahead of our competition," sounds outrageous. Take your well-earned bows, but be sure to give some of the credit to lady luck and good fortune. Reporters keep track of what you say when you are on your way up in case they should meet you on your way down. Be upbeat, but mind your words for the not-so-stellar days that are bound to follow.

And Finally

Do not indulge in spin. It has become a pejorative word for good reason. "Spin" or "spinning" is propaganda through the repetition of a story line to shape or distort perception. It's used a lot in politics to "frame" the debate and to co-opt issues. The practice has been with us since "friends, Romans, countrymen," but the term came of age in the late seventies, marking a cynical departure from the spinning of yarns, as in storytelling.

Political spin was witchcrafted by Lee Atwater, the all-star practitioner who helped Ronald Reagan win reelection in 1984. Atwater was both friend and mentor to a young Republican organizer by the name of Karl Rove, the former chief of staff for George W. Bush. Rove and his counterparts in the Democratic Party are sometimes referred to as "spin doctors."

Marie Antoinette, Queen of France from 1774 to 1793, is the most famous victim of spin. It was said that when the queen learned her subjects were starving due to a shortage of bread, she replied without a hint of irony, "Qu'ils mangent de la brioche," (Let them eat cake). The defining moment seemed in keeping with the negative public image of "Madame Deficit," as she was known. Marie Antoinette was blamed for the country's financial woes because of her lavish spending on parties, furnishings, clothes, and elaborate headdresses.

Historians have come to the rescue of the much-maligned queen. Apparently she never said these words. Rather, it was propaganda created by media-savvy revolutionaries to brand Louis XVI's Austrian wife as haughty and cruel. In fact, the phrase was recorded in *The Confessions of Jean-Jacques Rousseau*. The book was written several years

Arthur Schopenhauer's *The Art of Always Being Right: Thirty Eight Ways to Win When You Are Defeated* reads like the German philosopher's primer on spin, circa 1831. One trick calls for the use of jargon or gobbledygook. "If [your opponent] is secretly conscious of his own weakness and accustomed to hear much that he does not understand and to make as though he did, you can easily impose upon him by some serious fooling that sounds very deep or learned."

before the teenage princess even arrived in France. Too bad, history's most famous sound bite has stuck to Marie Antoinette, tarnishing her reputation to this day.

Interviews Are Not the Time for Original Thinking

Interviews can be intellectually stimulating. After all, reporters can be bright and engaging people. But a media interview is not the time to explore your belief system or other areas of thought. Nor is it a meditative exercise. Presidential candidate Jimmy Carter wrapped up his interview with *Playboy* magazine; then he took one more question. His answer would have far-reaching consequences. A decade or so later, Bill Clinton was asked to reveal his preference in underwear.

From Plains to Playboy

*I have looked on a lot of women with lust. I've committed
adultery in my heart many times. This is something that God
recognized I will do—and I have done—and God forgives me
for it.*
—Jimmy Carter

In the months leading up to the 1976 U.S. presidential
election, a throng of journalists was vying for time with
Jimmy Carter, the one-term governor from Georgia. Even as
Americans were asking "Jimmy who?" this soft-spoken fellow with a southern accent had blazed through a string of
primary victories. He used his biography as a "born-again
Christian" to color his messages about honesty and trust—
ideals that would define his campaign.

Americans were still reeling from the Watergate scandal
that led to the resignation of President Richard Nixon and
the pardon by his successor, Gerald Ford. Public sentiment,
which had cooled considerably for the Republican Party, had
shifted to the peanut farmer who captured the Democratic

Lust not after her beauty in
thine heart; neither let her
take thee with her eyelids.
—Proverbs 6:25, The Bible,
King James Version

nomination. Carter's campaign revolved around him not
being from Washington, not being a lawyer, and not being
the kind of man to lie. But Carter's religious testimonials
drew skeptics. People wondered how much his Baptist faith
would influence policy. Mindful of this, Carter's strategists
moved to protect his lead against President Ford. With the
aim to position him as principled, though hardly a prude,

they granted *Playboy* magazine's request for an interview.

Robert Scheer, a former managing editor of *Ramparts Magazine*, was on assignment for *Playboy*. He planned to connect the dots between Carter's public and private lives to uncover the man.

It was the morning of July 21, 1976, and Carter had just finished a session with a crew from *Reader's Digest*. Scheer and editor Barry Golson arrived at his Plains home as the *Digest* team was leaving. After saying hello to Carter's wife Rosalynn, the two men were led to the family's living room. Carter, dressed casually in jeans and work boots, sat in an armchair as the journalists set up the recorder. The pressing topic for *Playboy* was Carter's religious faith and its role in the formation of his political beliefs.

Sure, the reason most of us started reading *Playboy* was for the girls. But when the history of American magazines is written, people who said "I read it for the articles" will have the last laugh. As will Hugh Hefner, who told a reunion of Playmates in 1979, "Without you, I'd be the publisher of a literary magazine."
—Charles Taylor, "When Playboy was hot," Salon.com, October 9, 2002

SCHEER: *We've heard that you pray twenty-five times a day. Is that true?*

CARTER: *I've never counted. I've forgotten who asked me that, but I'd say that on an eventful day, you know, it's something like that.*

SCHEER: *When you say an eventful day, do you mean you pray as a kind of pause, to control your blood pressure and relax?*

CARTER: *Well, yes. If something happens to me that is a little disconcerting, if I feel trepidation, if a thought comes into my head of animosity or hatred toward someone, then I just kind of say a brief silent prayer.*

SCHEER: *One reason people might be quizzical is that you have a sister, Ruth, who is a faith healer. The association of politics with faith healing is an idea many find disconcerting.*

CARTER: *I don't even know what political ideas Ruth has had, and for the people to suggest I'm under the hold of my sister—or any other person—is a complete distortion of fact.*

Scheer continued to press Carter on other topics, including his views on homosexuality and judicial appointments. He was testing just how much of Carter's perspective was filtered through his Baptist lens. The candidate became frustrated by attempts to pin him down as a would-be moralist-in-chief leading with the cross.

The phrase, "Separation of Church and State" was born from a general interpretation of the Establishment Clause of the First Amendment of the United States Constitution, intended to protect the church from the state—not the other way around.

SCHEER: *We'd like to ask a blunt question: Isn't it just these views about what's "sinful" and what's "immoral" that contribute to the feeling that you might get a call from God, or get inspired and push the wrong button? More realistically, wouldn't we expect a puritanical tone to be set in the White House if you were elected?*

CARTER: *Harry Truman was a Baptist. Some people get very abusive about the Baptist faith. ... The main thing is that we don't think we're better than anyone else. We are taught not to judge other people.*

One hour later, press aide Rex Granum signaled that Carter was running late. The men wrapped up and everyone moved toward the front door. It was at that moment that the journalists almost apologetically explained their reasons for dwelling so much on the question of faith. In the same breath, Scheer "tossed off" what he later called a "seemingly casual" question.

SCHEER: *Do you feel you've reassured people with this interview, people who are uneasy about your religious beliefs, who wonder if you're going to make a rigid, unbending president?*

As Carter took time to reply, one of the men signaled to him that they were recording and he nodded his assent. Then came the moment Carter would long regret.

CARTER: *What Christ taught about most was pride, that one person should never think he was any better than anybody else [...]. I try not to commit a deliberate sin. I recognize that I'm going to do it anyhow, because I'm human and I'm tempted. And Christ set some almost impossible standards for us. Christ said, "I tell you that anyone who looks on a woman with lust has in his heart already committed adultery." I've looked on a lot of women with lust. I've committed adultery in my heart many times. This is something that God recognizes I will do—and I have done it—and God forgives me for it [...]. Christ says don't consider yourself better than someone else because one guy screws a whole bunch of women while the other guy is loyal to his wife. The guy who's loyal to his wife ought not to be condescending or proud because of the relative degree of sinfulness.*

It was dynamite. Just as the magazine's editors anticipated, Carter's off-the-wall musings astonished Americans. It made the November 1976 issue of *Playboy* a hot seller. Previews of the interview landed in newspapers in late September as Carter was slipping in polls. Few Americans expected such language or imagery to be conveyed in that forum by a man who held dear to his Christian values. Of the estimated 7.2 million *Playboy* readers, most no doubt were surprised to see Carter sharing space with a nude centerfold.

Carter's political pollster, Pat Caddell, explained that he

The November 1976 issue of *Playboy* featured Playmate Patti McGuire on the cover, with a bold headline that read, "NOW, THE REAL JIMMY CARTER ON POLITICS, RELIGION, THE PRESS AND SEX IN AN INCREDIBLE PLAYBOY INTERVIEW."

"used language that was germane to his world, like we all do." A *New York Times* editorial said of the confession, "Some journalists correctly saw the conversation as a warning sign of the future direction of American politics … the beginning of the erosion of the legitimate boundaries of private lives and intimate feeling have begun."

The interview came up at the first-ever vice presidential debate on October 15 between Republican Senator Bob Dole and Democratic Senator Walter Mondale. Dole attempted to capitalize on the Carter controversy, saying, "I couldn't understand frankly why he was in Playboy magazine, but we'll give him the bunny vote."

Carter lost supporters. His slight lead over Ford dissipated, then reappeared after the candidates' final debate, and lasted long enough to give him a slim victory. In 1989, Carter admitted to PBS's Jim Lehrer that his *Playboy* musings were a "devastating blow" to his campaign and almost cost him the presidency. Today the *Playboy* interview is seen as the archetypical event of the campaign.

The problem is that we are no longer certain about what public or private life really is. Private life has become politicized; public life has become suffused with private passions.
—Edward Rothstein, "Connections; Culture Rears Its Head in the Public-Private Debate," *New York Times*, September 28, 1998

Mastering Rule 6

Remember, originality in interviews is rarely rewarded. An interview is a time for facts, arguments, and considered opinions. It is not the occasion for out-of-the-box thinking on any subject. Nor is it the time to deal with hypothetical questions—or anything else you have not thought about beforehand.

Don't assume the interview is over because the reporter closes his notebook or turns off the recorder. The interview is over when you see the reporter actually leave the building or get into a car. There have been countless examples of people making remarks that they assumed were off the record while standing at the elevator, at the door, and even in the restroom. Why do so many people go off message at the end of an otherwise successful interview? Most of the time they are so relieved the "ordeal" is over they let their guard down. But the interview is never over for journalists while you are in their sights.

Do not underestimate what a crisis that interview and the "lust in my heart" caused Carter. It almost derailed the entire Carter campaign. They were in havoc over it.
—Douglas Brinkley, *American Experience*, PBS, November 2002

By all means, allow a recording device if asked. Many reporters use them to ensure more accurate note-taking. There is nothing sinister about this practice. It underscores the need for interview subjects to stay on point. However, a recording makes it more difficult for the interviewee to later claim that he was misquoted. The men had indicated to Carter that he was being taped, which was the ethical thing to do.

Don't waste time thinking of everything you could be asked.
Prepare for the half dozen most difficult interview questions. Next prepare for the six most obvious, including gift questions and softballs. (A "gift" question is a genuinely easy question, such as "tell us something about your company," whereas a "softball" is an easy question that could still trip you up.) Then focus your mind on the story you want to see with your name.

Game Face Conduct

Resist the temptation to exercise your intellectual creativity when responding to questions. Interviews are encounters requiring skill centered on messages. It makes little sense to reach for original thoughts when your words are being recorded for posterity. Resist a show of vanity or one-upmanship. The time to be inventive is before the interview, as you map a compelling storyline for your audience. During the interview, stick with the plan.

And Finally

The open microphone is a gift that keeps on giving (to the news cycle). Highlights include Vice President Dick Cheney's "Yeah, big time," reply to President George W. Bush's reference to a *New York Times* reporter as a "major-league asshole" during the 2004 presidential campaign. Bush later said he regretted the "private moment." Jesse Jackson also had regrets when he made a too-crude-to-print remark about what he would do to Barack Obama's private parts. He assumed he was "off-mic" while waiting to be interviewed by Fox News during the 2008 presidential race.

A more serious incident occurred only days before the 2010 national election in Britain. During a walkabout,

It was on this date that Bill Clinton discussed his underwear with the American people (briefs, not boxers, as it turned out). Why would the leader of the free world unburden himself like this? Why not? In television's increasingly postmodern world, all texts—serious and sophomoric—swirl together in the same discontinuous field of experience. To be sure, Mr. Clinton made his disclosure because he had been asked to do so by a member of the MTV generation, not because he felt a sudden need to purge himself.
—Roderick P. Hart and Mary Triece, "April 20, 1993: Bill Clinton's MTV Appearance," Museum of Broadcast Communications website

Prime Minister Gordon Brown began chatting with a lady, Gillian Duffy, who was voicing concern about immigrants flocking into the country from Eastern Europe. He soon bid her a warm farewell. But once inside the car, Brown's tone changed dramatically. "That was a disaster," he declared. "They should never have put me with that woman. Whose idea was that? Ridiculous." He worried about the coverage of his conversation with "just a sort of bigoted woman who said she used to be Labour." Unfortunately Brown was still wearing a Sky News microphone as his Jaguar departed, his very public criticism of a voter audible.

The next day Brown, trailed by dozens of reporters, turned up on Duffy's doorstep to apologize. Assume all microphones are open, broadcasting you live and uncensored!

We used to ask our presidents about great issues of war and peace. We ask President Clinton about his underwear. Worse, he gives us an answer.
—William F. Buckley, *National Review*, November 11, 1996

Beware the "Innocent" Question

The interview moment is almost as famous as Senator Edward Kennedy, the man dubbed the "Last Prince of Camelot." After the deaths of his brothers, President John F. Kennedy and Senator Robert F. Kennedy, came great expectations, chiefly the hope that Teddy would run for president. In an in-depth interview with CBS News, Kennedy showed great resolve in facing tough questions on his fear of assassination, his troubled marriage, his drinking, and the tragedy on the island of Chappaquiddick. But why was he at a loss when asked the *one* question he should have expected?

The Prince of Ambivalence

*Well, I'm—were I to make the announcement, and to run, the
reasons that I would run is because I have a great belief in
this country, that it is—there's more natural resources than any
nation of the world.*
—Edward Kennedy

In 1979, almost twenty years after the election of John F.
Kennedy, the popularity of forty-seven-year-old Edward
Kennedy had people convinced that he, too, was destined
for the White House. First he would have to get the nomination away from the incumbent, Democratic President Jimmy
Carter, whom Kennedy publicly supported. Immediately
after the senator signaled he was considering a run for president, calls to his Washington, D.C., office doubled to one
thousand a day. The American public had been waiting.

As the momentum was building, CBS News expressed interest in producing a one-hour program on the heir, husband,
and father of three. Two interviews would be conducted
by the network's chief congressional correspondent, Roger
Mudd, who was also a family friend. The men sat down in
Kennedy's Cape Cod home for the encounter. Kennedy was
soon uncomfortable with Mudd's line of questioning and
quick follow-ups, especially about the July 18, 1969 fatali-
ty on the island of Chappaquiddick, Massachusetts. That
night, Kennedy attended a party for a group of women who
had served on Robert Kennedy's presidential campaign. On

Ambivalence: simultaneous
and contradictory attitudes
or feelings (as attraction and
repulsion) toward an object,
person, or action.
—*Merriam-Webster's
Collegiate Dictionary,*
11th Edition

departing, Kennedy gave a ride to a twenty-eight-year-old woman named Mary Jo Kopechne. After driving a short distance, Kennedy turned his 1967 Oldsmobile Delmont onto a dirt road, then off a bridge, plunging the car into the dark waters of Poucha Pond. Kennedy managed to escape, but his passenger remained trapped in the car. He didn't report the accident until ten hours later. Under Mudd's intense probe, for the first time in an interview, Kennedy talked about leaving the scene of the accident, and leaving Kopechne to die.

MUDD: *Do you think Senator, that ... anybody really will ever believe your explanation of Chappaquiddick?*
KENNEDY: *Oh there's ... the problem is ... I found the conduct ah ... the behavior almost beyond belief myself. ... That ... that happens to be the way it was.*
MUDD: *You have said the physical trauma of that accident ... bears really no relationship to the pressures that are brought on by decisions of public policy that you are required to make as senator, they are separate. But what guarantee does a citizen have or what assurance does a citizen have that in the future you would not again act as you said, irresponsibly and inexplicably, when your own career came into conflict with the public's right to know?*
KENNEDY: *Well, I didn't make that distinction. I was asked a series of questions where others drew that conclusion. But what I pointed out is that the circumstances, that particular evening did involve physical trauma, did involve enormous, in the sense of loss ... in terms of the life of an individual. ... And, ... what I have recognized basically as a ... irresponsible behavior in not reporting the accident earlier. ... I have served in the United States Senate, for a position [sic] of 17 years, I have taken positions, I have spoken on issues, I have spoken on*

questions, and there's been other factors which have impacted my life and people will have to make that judgment.

Afterwards, a shaken Kennedy told aides that he had been blindsided by Mudd's line of questioning, describing the interview as "a disaster." According to Kennedy, he called and asked Mudd for "another crack at it."

In the second interview on October 12, 1979, this time from Kennedy's office in the nation's capital, the focus shifted to his achievements as a senator and his political ambitions. Then Mudd threw Kennedy a softball question.

MUDD: *Why do you want to be President?*
KENNEDY: *Well, I'm—were I to make the announcement, and to run, the reasons that I would run is because I have a great belief in this country, that it is—there's more natural resources than any nation of the world; there's the greatest technology of any country in the world; the greatest capacity for innovation in the world; and the greatest political system in the world. And yet I see at the current time that most of the industrial nations of the world are exceeding us in terms of productivity, are doing better than us in terms of meeting the problems of inflation; that they're dealing with their problems of energy and their problems of unemployment. ... It just seems to me that this nation can cope and deal with its problems in a way that it has in the past; we're facing complex issues and problems in this nation at this time that we have faced similar challenges at other times. And the energies and the resourcefulness of this nation, I think, should be focused on these problems in a way that brings a sense of restoration—in this country by its people to—in dealing with the problems that we face: primarily the issues of the economy,*

the problems of inflation, and the problems of—energy. And—I
would basically feel that—that it's imperative for this country
to either move forward; that it can't stand still or otherwise it
moves backward.

Not recognizing a germ of an answer in the 246-word response, Mudd pressed on. He rephrased the question. Still, Kennedy did not get any closer to articulating his vision for the country. There were other bad or fragmented answers, but this was the one that counted.

The two interviews were edited together and ran in an hour-long "CBS Reports" documentary, "Teddy," which aired on November 4, 1979. The attempt at scrutiny was familiar, but this time Kennedy had been forced to give an account of himself, with Chappaquiddick as the moral frame of his character.

On November 7, three days after the documentary aired, Kennedy announced his candidacy. His incoherent response to *the* question became the focus of unrelenting media criticism. Even those journalists who had been looking favorably to Camelot redux wondered if the defining moment had captured his sense of entitlement. "Teddy" allowed everyone a sober second look at the man who would be president. Anthony Lewis of the *New York Times* wrote, "Kennedy was stumbling, inarticulate, unconvincing. And not just on Chappaquiddick: His responses in general seemed to be those of a man unsure of the whys and wheres in his life—unsure who he was." As Edward Klein would write later in his book, *Edward Kennedy: The Dream That Never Died,* "Everything that followed the Mudd interview was anti-climactic."

Almost overnight, the unfavorable coverage and questions about Kennedy's ability to lead slowed his campaign.

The Kennedy myth had been perpetuated, even if unintentionally, by television. There was a special irony, therefore, when television turned on Ted Kennedy.
—John Corry, "TV View; TV Will Recall the Kennedy Years," *New York Times,* November 6, 1983

As a candidate, he was inconsistent. Soon, more primaries were lost to rivals than won. In August 1980, he ended his bid for the presidency with the memorable "the dream shall never die" speech at the Democratic National Convention that nominated President Jimmy Carter. While Kennedy would retain a place in the hearts of the American people, gone was the sense of inevitability.

For Mudd, the memory of the encounter remained vivid: "And suddenly I said, 'Ok why do you want to be president?' And the answer was, 'Well, because the sky is so blue and the grass is so green and the water's so cold' is basically what he said, and the answer did not make sense. And it suddenly occurred to people that maybe the senator didn't know why he wanted to be president or maybe he hadn't thought about it," he said in a 1999 C-Span interview.

What it did was enable the political journalists of the country to write really critical pieces about him, and it enabled them to watch out for and to be aware of this strange inarticulateness that he was carrying.
—Roger Mudd, *Booknotes*, C-Span, June 6, 1999

A "Roger Mudd Moment" would later describe a self-inflicted injury to an interview subject who fails to prepare for an obvious question.

The Mudd-Kennedy encounter would take on iconic status. Kennedy disputed the facts until the end of his life and in his memoir, *True Compass*, published posthumously in 2009. According to Kennedy, questions about his candidacy were supposed to have been off limits and Mudd, a veteran reporter, came to interview him about his family's love of the sea.

In his book, *The Place To Be: Washington, CBS and the Glory Days of Television News*, published in 2008, Mudd states that the interview was to be on Kennedy, the man and senator.

Kennedy couldn't claim he was misquoted, as his words were captured on film. Instead he raised questions about

Mudd's tactics and journalistic ethics. Still, his rambling response was evidence of something unresolved that led him to turn an obvious question into a long remembered, and much debated, defining moment.

Mastering Rule 7

Don't preempt yourself before an important announcement.
If there is a possibility of a conflict, hold off. Anyone interviewing Ted Kennedy would have asked if he was planning a presidential run. Kennedy should have delayed the interview until he was ready to declare his intentions.

Interview subjects can lack knowledge, but they should not appear to lack self-knowledge. Watch out for "puffballs," those not-so-innocent questions. Like softballs they can be tricky because they tend to be personal. It is precisely because they are not "hardballs" that a bad answer can be damaging, as it was for Kennedy. In 2008, Sarah Palin danced around a question on the "Bush Doctrine" during an interview with Charles Gibson of ABC News. Although she was the Republican Party's vice-presidential candidate, Palin's response caused barely a stir because few viewers were familiar with the term used to describe the policy of preemptive military strike. But when CBS's Katie Couric asked Palin to name a newspaper or magazine that helped to shape her "world view," Palin couldn't name one and the moment defined her candidacy. Palin complained that she had been ambushed. Few agreed, including her campaign's chief strategist Steve Schmidt, who commented, "In my view there was nothing that Katie Couric asked in that interview that was unfair."

Softball: a sport similar to baseball played on a small diamond with a ball that is larger than a baseball and that is pitched underhand; *also:* the ball used in this game.
—*Merriam-Webster's Collegiate Dictionary,* 11th Edition

Mudd threw another softball, and Kennedy swung and missed again. On the simple question that would define him and his political destiny, Kennedy had no clue.
—Chris Whipple, "The Day the Presidency Was Lost" ABC News, August 31, 2009

Remember, unlike softballs, a "gift" question is really a gift. Gift questions are open-ended questions handed to subjects on a platter. They can act as an opener to soften the tone or as a closer after the damage has been done. Often to finish an interview, the reporter will ask, "Do you have anything to add?" or "Have I forgotten anything?" quite straightforwardly. This is the time to repeat your most important message. There have been interview subjects who have actually replied, "No, I don't."

You have the right to stop an interview at any time. That's a far better option than to continue saying things that you don't want to see broadcast. No need to worry about hurting the reporter's feelings. The same thing goes for print interviews. Don't wait until after the material has been gathered to complain, expecting that it won't be used. If the quotes or sound bites exist, they can be used any time. And consider this: All materials gathered during the development of a story are the property of the news organization, not the reporter. This means that other reporters and producers have access to your words for future use.

Game Face Conduct

When the stakes are high, consider the possibility of your own ambivalence. The critics agreed that Kennedy should have expected the question, but they disagreed on the reason for his verbal malfunction. Some said it was because he wasn't thoughtful or mature, while others claimed Kennedy lacked vision. Mudd came to believe that Kennedy felt he had a divine right to the job as the inheritor of Camelot. But there is another possible explanation for Kennedy's to-be-or-not-be moment: he was conflicted. Note, Kennedy didn't

I don't want to be known—and don't think I should be known—as the man who brought Ted Kennedy down. I was a man who did an interview with him that was not helpful.
—Roger Mudd, "Ted Kennedy: The Interview," Boston.com, 2009

give a bad answer—he avoided the question completely. He sounded like a man who on that particular day wasn't sure he wanted to be president, though it was expected. The Senate must have felt like home to Kennedy who, as a boy, had gone to ten schools in thirteen years. During his 47-year tenure he would see many presidents come and go.

And Finally

History seemed to repeat itself in 2008, nearly thirty years later, when Caroline Kennedy became the front runner to replace Hillary Clinton, the senator from New York. Kennedy, the daughter of President John F. Kennedy, had an impressive record of giving back. Still, many thought her unqualified, and after a series of blistering interviews with the *New York Times,* she failed to change their minds. Kennedy, a lawyer and author, didn't seem to know how to make her case or what to reveal after decades of having to guard her privacy. Her constant repetition of "you know" and "kind of" made her sound unsure and uncommitted. She stumbled badly when she was asked why she wanted the job. An ailing Ted Kennedy is known to have played a crucial role in encouraging his niece to seek the appointment. Caroline Kennedy's ambivalent responses wiped away her many advantages, forcing her to withdraw from consideration. In contrast, Kennedy breezed through her 2013 confirmation hearings after she was named the U.S. ambassador to Japan.

He ignites every debate and issue he ever decided to touch. Let no one ever accuse this man of simply punching the clock.
—Republican Senator Mitch McConnell, upon Senator Kennedy casting his 15,000th vote, September 4, 2007

For years, reporters assigned to cover Ted Kennedy had advance copies of his obituary with them, figuring that, if his compulsive eating and drinking did not get him, some nut with a gun might. But he had defied the odds. Of all the Kennedy brothers, only he had lived long enough, in the words of the Irish poet William Butler Yeats, to "comb grey hair."
—Edward Klein, *Ted Kennedy: The Dream That Never Died,* 2009

Always Concede the Obvious

Before you begin an interview, know what you will and won't give up, or you may find yourself defending ground that's already been lost. If the situation is particularly serious, as it was for Congressman Gary Condit, offer up the damaging information early so that you can move on to other things. In interviews, as in life, it's where you end up that matters.

Foolish Innocent or Cagey Monster?

And I think the American people, and the people watching out there understand. I think they understand that ... that I'm entitled to some of my privacy. My family's entitled to some of their privacy. And certainly the Levys are, as well.
—Gary Condit

Chandra Levy was last seen on April 30, 2001, at a Washington, D.C., health club, where she had gone to discontinue her membership. Having reached the end of an internship at the U.S. Federal Bureau of Prisons, she was preparing to return home to attend her graduation at the University of California. The next day Levy disappeared. Five days later, her anxious parents, Dr. Robert and Susan Levy, called D.C. police. Soon they were in the nation's capital, demanding answers and drawing media attention with talk about a missing intern and a married congressman.

The search for information on Levy's whereabouts led her family and police to Congressman Gary Condit, a Democrat, whose district included Levy's hometown of Modesto, California. Levy met Condit in the fall of 2000 on a visit to Capitol Hill. They began dating in secret. Soon it was an open secret, as Chandra told one close friend and then another about her new boyfriend.

Overnight Condit, the affable fifty-three-year-old husband and father, was the center of a media storm as rumors swirled about his relationship with the missing

"Not a Suspect"; Rep. Condit Couldn't Have Played This Any Worse if He Tried
—headline, *Washington Post*, July 8, 2001

twenty-four-year-old. Condit refused to be interviewed. In his public statement, Condit referred to Levy as "a good friend" and he contributed $10,000 to a reward for her safe return. But to investigators, Condit was evasive on the nature of his relationship with Levy. The Congressman left the official denial of an affair to his chief of staff.

Condit's silence added to the mystery, creating the impression that he had something to hide. Meanwhile, Levy's parents were giving interviews and keeping him in the news. By mid-May, Condit was linked to the disappearance itself. Reporters and camera crews began camping outside his home in Ceres, California. In the Washington, D.C., neighborhood of Adams-Morgan, they herded near the entrance of his condo to catch him in the mornings. Others arrived throughout the day, anxious to make news as they headed into the dog days of summer.

Police said repeatedly that Condit was not a suspect. Off the record, they complained about Condit's strategy of silence. On June 7, the *Washington Post* reported that, according to sources, Levy had spent at least one night at Condit's apartment. Soon there were leaks about another extramarital affair. There was pressure on Condit to come clean about the relationship, which was now the media's main focus along with the disappearance itself.

A June 8 editorial in his hometown newspaper, the *Modesto Bee*, couldn't have been more direct: "Five weeks of silence is enough. Condit has a duty to publicly clarify his relationship with Levy." On July 6, Linda Zamsky, Levy's aunt, released a bombshell statement. "From my many conversations with her, it was clear, without a doubt, that they were involved in an intimate relationship. She described, in detail, some of their bedroom encounters," stated Zamsky.

When tabloids turned the tragedy of Chandra's disappearance into a spectacle and rumors were reported as facts, I decided that I would not discuss my private life in the media.
—Gary Condit, letter to constituents of the 18th Congressional District, August 23, 2001

Condit denied that he and Levy were planning a future together, telling the *Washington Post*, "I don't believe the aunt knows anything about me. I had no interest in starting a family and leaving my wife."

In his third interview with police, Condit finally admitted that the relationship with Levy was sexual. At this point, hopes were fading for her return. In the minds of many, she was presumed dead. Now the tabloids were full of murder plots and theories of how Condit may have killed Levy. Yet, there was absolutely no evidence linking him to her disappearance.

July brought more bad news for Condit: police searched his apartment, seized his phone records, requested a sample of his DNA, and asked to interview his wife. On July 12, 2001, Republican Bob Barr became the first member of Congress to call for Condit's resignation. The next day, *Time* magazine selected him as its Person of the Week because, as reporter Frank Pellegrini put it, "Condit's public pose—the politician's equivalent of pulling your coat over your head—has left the hordes one of two impressions: of a cowardly (and foolish) innocent or a cagey monster."

It was time for Condit to fight back—with words.

Fox News called it "the biggest 'get' in television news since ABC's Barbara Walters nabbed Monica Lewinsky." Condit agreed to give Connie Chung of ABC's *Primetime* an exclusive interview. Chung was not known as a hard-hitting interviewer in the Mike Wallace mode. But on August 23, 2001, in a live, nationwide broadcast, Chung got right to the point and stayed there.

CHUNG: *Congressman Condit, do you know what happened to Chandra Levy?*

CONDIT: *No, I do not.*

CHUNG: *Did you have anything to do with her disappearance?*

CONDIT: *No, I didn't.*

CHUNG: *Did you say or do anything that could have caused her to drop out of sight?*

CONDIT: *You know, Chandra and I never had a cross word.*

CHUNG: *Do you have any idea if there was anyone who wanted to harm her?*

CONDIT: *No.*

CHUNG: *Did you cause anyone to harm her?*

CONDIT: *No.*

CHUNG: *Did you kill Chandra Levy?*

CONDIT: *No, I did not.*

CHUNG: *Can you describe your relationship? What exactly was your relationship with Chandra?*

CONDIT: *Well, I met Chandra ... last October. And we became very close. I met her in Washington, D.C.*

CHUNG: *Very close, meaning?*

CONDIT: *We had a close relationship. I liked her very much.*

CHUNG: *May I ask you, was it a sexual relationship?*

CONDIT: *Well, Connie, I've been married for 34 years, and I've not been a ... perfect man, and I've made my share of mistakes. But out of respect for my family, and out of a specific request from the Levy family, I think it's best that I not get into those details, about Chandra Levy.*

The congressman continued while insisting on his right to privacy. Chung returned to the question on everyone's mind.

CHUNG: *Would you like to ... tell the truth about the relationship with her?*

CONDIT: *I've told you and responded to the relationship question. And I think the American people, and the people watching out there understand. I think they understand that ... that I'm entitled to some of my privacy. My family is entitled to some of their privacy. And certainly the Levys as well.*

Finally, Chung asked Condit one question he seemed keen to answer.

CHUNG: *Can you survive, can your career, your marriage survive this?*
CONDIT: *Well, my family's intact. It's going to take more than the news media ... with its innuendos, half-truths, unnamed sources, to split my family up.*

An estimated twenty-three million viewers tuned in to hear what Condit had to say, including the Levy family. Within an hour of the broadcast, their lawyer, Billy Martin, appeared on ABC's *Nightline* with Ted Koppel. He repudiated Condit's claim that the Levys "made a specific request" for him to honor their privacy and not offer details of his relationship with their daughter. "I wish he would answer the question," Martin told Koppel. "What was his relationship with Chandra?"

Before the broadcast, Condit mailed two-hundred thousand letters to his constituents advising them that it was time to speak out. "I will be interviewed on television and hopefully I will be able to answer questions that help people understand," he said. But the public relations offensive was a failure. As Jim Rutenberg reported in the *New York Times* the next day, "Condit finally publicly faced some questions. But he left most of them unanswered, almost

I can't believe he's not being more candid. I can't believe he's not taking responsibility.
—Dick Gephardt, Democratic house minority leader, "How Not To Build A Reputation," *Time*, August 26, 2001

guaranteeing that the 'media circus' he derided during the interview would continue."

Most devastating was Tom Shales in the *Washington Post.* "Condit was not paid for the interview, but if he had been, Chung should have demanded her money back right there on the air," he wrote. Condit's uncooperative stance continued to stir debate.

The destruction of the World Trade Center's twin towers on September 11, 2001, blew the Levy-Condit story off the media map. Condit pursued his reelection bid but he lost the March 2002 primary election to his former protégé and aide, Dennis Cardoza. After thirteen years in congress, Condit was rejected by voters. *Washingtonian* magazine suggested that Condit's lawyer, Abbie Lowell, "may have overplayed his hand when he allowed an unrepentant client to do an interview with Connie Chung."

In a lengthy feature in *Esquire* magazine in September 2002, Condit lashed out at the media and Connie Chung, saying, "She wasn't getting anything out of me; she wasn't going to break me, no way. … And she asked the one question like ten times, maybe twenty times."

Lost on Condit was the possibility that his failure to address *that* question led to his undoing. Condit will never know if he could have survived the affair and Levy's disappearance if he had given up the one thing the situation demanded. Instead Condit held fast to something already lost—and for too long.

An innocent man looking to salvage his reputation would be all empathy and earnestness, not defiant half-answers or the lawyerly "Don't say more than you're asked" stance, and certainly not a taut smile when asked whether you've killed a "close friend."
—Michael Duffy and Nancy Gibbs, "How Not to Build a Reputation," *Time,* August 26, 2001

Rep. Charles B. Rangel, a New York Democrat, called Condit's behavior "embarrassing." But he questioned whether the Ethics Committee has sufficient justification to conduct an investigation. "What do we charge him with?" Rangel asked on *Fox News Sunday.* "A bad television performance?"
—Richard Simon, "Political, legal woes deepen for Condit," *Baltimore Sun,* August 27, 2001

Mastering Rule 8

Always concede the obvious. An unwillingness to acknowledge what reasonable people assume damages your credibility, and fast. The denial of mistakes, bad conduct, poor earnings, or in this case an affair doesn't change the facts or make the problem go away. It simply delays your recovery.

Never fall behind the news when the subject is you. Within twenty-four hours after he learned of Chandra Levy's disappearance, Condit should have made a statement to the media, acknowledging his affair with the young woman. He should have apologized to his family and his constituents, and pledged to cooperate fully with investigators. With that, Condit would have ended the worst day of his life with one giant step forward.

Don't ignore the likability factor when telling your side of the story. Condit's refusal to speak of Levy intensified interest in the affair and hardened public sentiment against him. For months prior to his appearance on *Primetime Live*, Condit had been portrayed in the media as uncooperative and uncaring. He cemented that impression by conducting himself as a hostile witness at his own trial, which came in the form of a media interview.

Remember—how you manage your personal history speaks volumes. Almost everyone has something they regret. Old relationships and memberships may no longer be relevant.

CALLER: Any idea why the Levy case continues to garner such national and local media interest?
KURTZ: Two words: Gary Condit. It's Chandra's alleged romantic entanglement with a member of Congress who has not answered a public question about his "good friend" for two months now that keeps the press hot on the trail.
—Howard Kurtz, "Media Backtalk with Howard Kurtz," washingtonpost.com, July 2, 2001

Previously expressed beliefs, when brought to light, may cause embarrassment as you no longer hold them (or because you still do). When asked to explain, it's not helpful to go on the defensive. The skill is to distance yourself from your less-evolved self with grace.

News is conflicts, controversies, and inconsistencies. Condit became a magnet for media attention by attracting all three. First, he got drawn into a public relations war with the grieving family. Second, after years of telling voters that he was a leader, Condit portrayed himself as a victim of the media. Third, though a public servant, he misled police. When Bill Clinton was in trouble for his relationship with an intern, Condit labeled the president's conduct "inexcusable and indefensible."

Tactic

In a crisis, focus on what you *can* control. Success demands action, not reaction. Be proactive or you will find yourself overtaken by events and the machination of others. Condit should have presented the facts to end speculation about his relationship with Levy. At the same time, Condit should have drawn up a plan to regain the trust of his constituents.

> The longer Gary kept silent, the worse it became. Shut out, the media laid siege. Inside the castle, desperation led to bad decisions, worse results.
> —Mike Sager, "The Final Days of Gary Condit," *Esquire*, September 2002

Game Face Conduct

It is unseemly to lay claim to high moral principles in public if your private conduct suggests otherwise. Condit's decision to brand himself as a responsible family man was at odds with his history. He spoke of honor, but what the public saw was a man dishonoring a grieving family and self-described "good friend" with his silence. Condit

At the 2010 trial, which convicted Ingmar Guandique of Chandra Levy's murder, Gary Condit was asked about the nature of his relationship with Chandra Levy. Condit replied, "I'm not going to respond." DNA taken from clothing in Levy's apartment and introduced as evidence confirmed the fact that she and Condit had shared an intimate relationship.

Guandique was granted a new trial in 2015. Less than a year later, the case against him was dismissed due to "unforeseen circumstances."

continued with the career-ending strategy before an audience of millions, turning his primetime interview into a long and awkward apology to his wife.

And Finally

Fawning or fierce, this is the age of the media interview. On-the-record exchanges create defining moments, igniting careers and often extinguishing them. The ubiquitous Q & A is an American invention. Horace Greeley (1811–1872), the journalist and politician who founded the once-mighty *New York Tribune* in 1841, is credited with its popularization. Greeley's 1859 interview with Brigham Young, the head of the Mormon Church, is said to be the first formal interview ever published. Meanwhile, over in England, where tabloid journalism was born, the interviewing trade was receiving bad press.

In 1869, the *Daily News* informed its readers, "A portion of the daily newspapers of New York are bringing the profession of Journalism into contempt, so far as they can, by a kind of toadyism or flunkeyism which they call 'interviewing.'" In 1886, the *Pall Mall Gazette* went further, declaring the practice "degrading to the interviewer, disgusting to the interviewee, and tiresome to the public." But the interview was here to stay.

Assume the Truth Will Come Out

If you go public with only half the story, the other half is
sure to follow. In the case of James Frey, the moment of
truth came after he reached the sweet spot on the Ferris
wheel of life. The author was sitting next to Oprah Winfrey,
and the two were deep in conversation about his memoir.
His was an apocalyptic tale of survival—hauntingly moving
and so real. Or was it? Winfrey, Frey would learn, could
forgive a drug addict and even a criminal, but not a liar and
a public deceiver.

Keeping Oprah Awake at Night

*I don't know if I wish I had put a disclaimer in it or if I had
just written about certain events in a different way.*
—James Frey

On October 26, 2005, Oprah Winfrey appeared before
television viewers as an avid fan of *A Million Little
Pieces*, a new memoir written by an emerging New York
author named James Frey. With heartfelt enthusiasm,
she named it the Oprah Book Club selection, making
Frey the first living author in three years to receive such
affirmation. It was also a departure, given the book's
coarse language and subject matter. Oprah's book club
hailed a membership in the millions. In its nine years,
it generated the purchasing power to transform obscure
books into bestsellers. The talk show entrepreneur was
the publishing world's biggest promoter.

A Million Little Pieces, Winfrey informed her audience,
was "like nothing you've ever read before." She and her staff
dedicated an entire show—aptly entitled "The Man Who
Kept Oprah Awake at Night"—to Frey. The author received
precious airtime to elaborate on his tale of alcohol and
drug addiction, crime, self-loathing, and redemption—all
described in graphic detail. As Frey told the host, "If I was
going to write a book that was true, and I was going to write
a book that was honest, then I was going to have to write
about myself in negative ways."

Whether I shall turn out to
be the hero of my own life,
or whether that station will
be held by anybody else,
these pages must show.
—Charles Dickens, *David
Copperfield*, 1850

Winfrey's endorsement was a heaven-send for Frey, a sad-faced, thirty-five-year-old recovering drug addict. His manuscript had attracted star publisher Nan A. Talese and he received an advance of $50,000. But it was the guest spot on *Oprah* that ensured the book's upward trajectory. For fifteen straight weeks after Winfrey's endorsement, his memoir remained at the top of the *New York Times* bestsellers' list for nonfiction paperbacks.

A Million Little Pieces was met with a shower of praise for its riveting style of storytelling. "Electrifying," "mesmerizing," and "unflinchingly honest," spouted reviewers. But a resounding crash would leave Frey's reputation in a million little pieces.

Two months after his appearance on *Oprah*, the now-famous author was approached by the investigative website The Smoking Gun. The internet sleuths went searching for a mug shot of Frey, who claimed to have been arrested thirteen times. On January 8, 2006, The Smoking Gun ran an exclusive based on a six-week investigation with the tongue-in-cheek headline "A Million Little Lies." It reported that the most sensational episodes in Frey's narrative were checked and re-examined and found to be untrue.

It seems James Frey was not as bad as bad could be. He had never, for example, broken a U.S. record for highest blood-alcohol level, nor was he a criminal "wanted in three states." Worse, Frey's claim that he was made the fall guy after his best friend and another girl were killed in a train wreck was a lie. He barely knew the real-life teenaged victims. The Smoking Gun concluded that "Frey appears to have fictionalized his past to propel and sweeten the book's already melodramatic narrative and help convince readers of his malevolence."

> They speak to me, make sense to me, reverberate within me, calm, ease, sedate, relax, still pacify me. They ring true and that is all that matters, the truth.
> —James Frey, on the *Tao Te Ching*, *A Million Little Pieces*, 2003

At first, Frey attempted to cover up his lies. He even threatened The Smoking Gun with a lawsuit before admitting the truth to the website's reporters. He acknowledged "taking steps around the time *A Million Little Pieces* was published in hardcover in 2003 to legally expunge court records related to the seemingly most egregious criminal activity of his lifetime," said the website. As for Winfrey, she, like millions of fans worldwide, didn't believe the accusations leveled against Frey.

Three days after the story broke, Frey was on CNN's *Larry King Live* responding to questions from viewers. Winfrey called the show defending him: "The underlying message of redemption in James Frey's memoir still resonates with me, and I know it resonates with millions of people who have read this book. ... To me, it seems to be much ado about nothing," she told King's audience. But the weight of publicity compelled Winfrey to get Frey back on her show.

On January 26, 2006, a grave-looking Winfrey confronted the author.

WINFREY: *I have to say it is difficult for me to talk to you because I feel duped. But more importantly, I feel that you betrayed millions of readers. I think it's such a gift to have millions of people read your work and that bothers me greatly. So now as I sit here today I don't know what is true and I don't know what isn't. So first of all, I wanted to start with The Smoking Gun report. ... I want to know, were they right?*
FREY: *I think most of what they wrote was accurate. Absolutely.*
WINFREY: *Okay.*
FREY: *I think they did a good job detailing some of the discrepancies between some of the actual facts of the events ...*

WINFREY: *What The Smoking Gun said was that you lied about the length of time that you spent in jail. How long were you in jail?*

FREY: *The Smoking Gun was right about that. I was in for a few hours.*

WINFREY: *Not 87 days?*

FREY: *Correct.*

WINFREY: *Why did you lie? Why did you lie about the time you spent in jail? Why did you do that?*

FREY: *I think one of the coping mechanisms I developed was sort of this image of myself that was greater, probably, than—not probably—that was greater than what I actually was. In order to get through the experience of the addiction, I thought of myself as being tougher than I was and badder than I was—and it helped me to cope. When I was writing the book ... instead of being introspective as I should have been, I clung to that image.*

WINFREY: *Or did you cling to that image because that's how you wanted to see yourself? Or did you cling to that image because that made a better book?*

FREY: *Probably both.*

Winfrey went through her checklist of Frey's falsehoods like a prosecutor at a murder trial. Frey, his expression mostly deadpan, served up qualified responses. For example, he was now fuzzy on the details of his brutally-etched account of the back-to-back root canal surgeries he endured without anesthesia while in rehab.

FREY: *I mean, once I talked to the person at the facility about it, you know, the book had been out for nine months. We'd already done a lot of the interviews about it. ... Since that time I struggled with the idea of it ..."*

WINFREY: *No, the lie of it. That's a lie. It's not an idea, James. That's a lie.*

Frey had originally pitched his book as fiction, but *A Million Little Pieces* was brought out as a memoir and marketed to readers as a true story. Winfrey was not visibly moved by Frey's predicament and kept up her questioning despite the awkwardness of the situation. Finally Winfrey asked Frey what he was willing to do to make amends.

WINFREY: *Do you now wish you had put a disclaimer in the book, James?*
FREY: *I don't know if I wish I had put a disclaimer in it or if I had just written about certain events in a different way. I think that would have been the more appropriate thing to do than putting in a disclaimer.*

People in the studio audience were floored by what they were witnessing. Their silence was broken by gasps, some boos, or a swell of applause whenever Winfrey cut Frey down to size with biting disapproval. He was paying the price for putting the celebrated interviewer in this position. But true to her signature style, Winfrey sent him off with words of encouragement. "Maybe this is the beginning of another kind of truth for you," she said.

Where the truth led, others followed. After the public dressing down, came condemnation from the industry. Frey's agent and publisher dropped him. Warner Brothers cancelled plans to base a film on his much-refuted memoir. Facing lawsuits, Frey and Random House reached a legal settlement, requiring them to offer refunds to consumers who felt cheated.

Frey's humiliating outing led to a mountain of media coverage. The book was subsequently published with an apology to readers. "My mistake, and it is one that I deeply regret, is writing about the person I created in my mind to help me cope," wrote Frey, "and not the person who went through the experience." After the fall, Frey became the poster child for literary deception, but *A Million Little Pieces* continued on its bestselling streak.

Frey could have written himself a different ending. After receiving the call from The Smoking Gun, he could have faced the truth and the inevitability of public exposure. Rather than deny, threaten, or cover up, Frey could have seized the moment in the spirit of the bold character he portrayed in his book. With that scenario, Frey would have called Winfrey and invited himself back onto her show.

He continues to be everyone's favorite punch line—however outlandish the comparison may be. When it was revealed in February that the author of a Holocaust-survival memoir was a Gentile and spent the war safely in Brussels, she was called the new Frey. When the author of a memoir about L.A. gang life turned out to be a nice middle-class suburban white girl, she was a new new Frey.
—Evgenia Peretz, "James Frey's Morning After," *Vanity Fair*, June 2008

Mastering Rule 9

**First The Denials,
Then The Admissions**

**William J. Clinton:
The President**

I want you to listen to me.
I'm going to say this again. I
did not have sexual relations
with that woman, Miss
Lewinsky.
—Bill Clinton, White House,
January 26, 1998

I did have a relationship
with Miss Lewinsky that was
not appropriate. In fact, it
was wrong. It constituted
a critical lapse in judgment
and a personal failure on my
part for which I am solely
and completely responsible.
—Bill Clinton in a televised
address to the nation,
August 17, 1998

Never lie or make misleading statements in an interview. The lie becomes Exhibit A in the court of public opinion and forever taints your reputation.

Remember, while the cover-up is not always worse than the crime, it is *always* a mistake. The second deception wipes away any benefit of the doubt as to character. It destroys trust.

Don't provoke the wrath of allies by clinging to falsehoods. During Frey's appearance on *Larry King Live*, Winfrey called in to defend him. Frey compromised her and other supporters by insisting he was the victim when he was not. Frey mounted an aggressive defense against The Smoking Gun exposé, daring to go online with the battle cry "So let the haters hate, let the doubters doubt, I stand by my book and my life." Frey was following the adage "The best defense is a good offense." Better to take the advice of political analyst David Gergen: "If you don't come clean early, it gets worse and worse."

Remember, when it comes to lies, size doesn't matter. In his post-exposé defense, Frey repeatedly stated that only eighteen of the 432 pages in his book contain "disputed events." It was hardly a defense, as his book was billed as a memoir. Frey's claim to be "shocked" by the uproar was a calculated attempt to blame the media attention for the problem rather than his conduct. Blaming the media is always a losing strategy.

Don't underestimate the source when you're the story. With the vast echo chamber of the Internet, it's a level playing field. Frey may have thought that he could trump The Smoking Gun web reporters by spinning his version of the story in primetime on CNN's *Larry King Live*. However, anyone with a computer is a fact-checker and a reporter. Today all media are big media and everything is in "the public domain."

Tactic

You can't fix a lie with a lie. What you can and should do is gain time while you develop a plan to correct the problem. Agree on a deadline for your response and honor it. While you owe the reporter a return call or email, you can choose to go public with the truth elsewhere. In any case, the quicker the flight from denial to acceptance, the better the odds for managing a negative situation. Set the record straight with the precision of a surgeon with no time to lose.

Game Face Conduct

Don't offer excuses when it's time to come clean. Frey lied in his book, he lied about the book, and then attempted to rationalize his deception. His reluctance to come clean made things worse. During the second interview with Winfrey, Frey still wasn't clear if he "wished" he had written about things differently (that is, told the truth) or written a disclaimer (that is, admit he made stuff up). Winfrey didn't humiliate Frey; he humiliated himself by leaving the

John Edwards: The Candidate

REPORTER: *Can you comment on the National Enquirer report on your secret meeting with your mistress and child?*

EDWARDS: *That's tabloid trash. They're full of lies. I'm here to talk about helping people.*
—John Edwards, at a press conference in Houston, Texas, July 23, 2008

In 2006, I made a serious error in judgment and conducted myself in a way that was disloyal to my family and to my core beliefs ... I had a liaison with another woman.
—John Edwards, statement, August 8, 2008

I know that it's not possible that this child could be mine because of the timing of events, so I know it's not possible.
—John Edwards, *Nightline*, ABC, August 8, 2008

I am Quinn's father. ... It was wrong for me ever to deny she was my daughter.
—John Edwards, statement, January 21, 2010

impression that he still wasn't sure if it was the lie, the cover up, or getting caught that was the problem.

Alex Rodriguez:
The Ball Player

COURIC: For the record, have you ever taken steroids, human growth hormones or any performance-enhancing substance?
RODRIGUEZ: No.
COURIC: Have you ever been tempted to use any of those things?
RODRIGUEZ: No.
—Katie Couric and Alex Rodriguez, *60 Minutes*, CBS, December 16, 2007

GAMMONS: You were asked if you ever used steroids, human growth hormones or other performance-enhancing substances. You said no, flat-out no. In your mind, that wasn't a lie?
RODRIGUEZ: At the time, Peter, I wasn't even being truthful with myself. How am I going to be truthful with Katie or CBS? Today, I'm here to tell the truth, and I feel good about that.
—Peter Gammons and Alex Rodriguez, ESPN, February 9, 2009

And Finally

No one should underestimate what it takes to lie during an interview. On the spot, the human brain can be counted on to forget what it was supposed to remember. Perhaps this is the reason television viewers are drawn to jailhouse interviews with convicted criminals proclaiming their innocence. Still, it was something of a first when Scott Peterson agreed to talk on the record—before he was even charged with first-degree murder. It had been four weeks since his pregnant wife, Laci Peterson, dissappeared in Modesto, California. Scott Peterson was the prime suspect when he agreed to speak with Diane Sawyer on ABC's *Good Morning America* in January 2003. In this and other interviews he gave, against the advice of his lawyers, Peterson maintained his innocence while he encouraged volunteers to continue their search for his wife.

SAWYER: *What kind of marriage was it?*
PETERSON: *God, the first word that comes to mind is, you know, glorious. I mean we took care of each other, very well. She was amazing. She is amazing.*

Peterson's correction was the problem. It would have been a natural "slip" to speak of Laci in the past tense given her suspicious disappearance. With his quick switch to the present tense, it was as if Peterson was saying to the audience, "*Oh, wait, I'm not supposed to know she's dead.*" Peterson did not testify at the trial but the *Good Morning America* interview was played for the jury to highlight discrepancies in his story. Peterson was convicted of murder in 2004.

In 2008, another high-profile murder suspect sat down for a pre-trial interview. Jody Arias gave yet another version of events leading up to the brutal murder of her former boyfriend, Travis Alexander. She told *Inside Edition*, "I witnessed Alexander being killed by two other individuals." The word "other" jumps out because it suggests she was really saying, two other people (who don't exist) besides me. In 2013, Arias was found guilty of first-degree murder.

Rob Ford:
The Mayor
City of Toronto
[2010–2014]

These allegations are ridiculous.
—Rob Ford, *Toronto Sun*, May 17, 2013

I cannot comment on a video that I have never seen or does not exist.
—Rob Ford, CBC News, May 24, 2013

Yes, I have smoked crack cocaine. ... Probably in one of my drunken stupors, approximately about a year ago.
—Rob Ford, *Toronto Star*, November 5, 2013

I just want to come out and tell you I saw the video. It's extremely embarrassing. The whole world is going to see it.
—Rob Ford, *Toronto Star*, November 7, 2013

Cultivate the Editor in Your Head

Kids say the darndest things and that's part of their charm. They have not learned to observe or censor their comments. We call that innocence. But when adults make stupid, hurtful, or inappropriate remarks, it is a serious matter. Along with the damage caused, it shows just how detached they are from their thought process. For a high-profile example we go to Toronto, where it's the mayor who had to say "I'm sorry"—twenty times.

Listening to What's Being Heard

What the hell do I want to go to a place like Mombasa?
Snakes just scare the hell out of me. I'm sort of scared about
going there, but the wife is really nervous. I just see myself in a
pot of boiling water with all these natives dancing around me.
—Mel Lastman

The Canadian flag was flying high in front of Toronto's City Hall on March 7, 2001, at the ceremony to mark the city's bid to host the 2008 Summer Olympic Games. Toronto had landed in third place for the 1996 Games, which went to Atlanta. This time, Toronto's Olympic Committee was certain that the country's largest city was ready. It boasted a sprawling waterfront along Lake Ontario and, above all, a large multicultural population. Toronto's motto, "Diversity Our Strength," was tailor made.

The bid team was busy preparing for a five-day visit from the evaluation commission of the International Olympic Committee (IOC). The team also had to deal with the concerns of local groups, who viewed the Olympics as an expensive distraction from the city's more pressing business. "Bread not circuses" was their motto.

China was favored to win, having lost the 2000 Games to Sydney by two votes. After Beijing, Toronto and Paris were the strongest contenders. By early June, Toronto's prospects to host the 2008 Games brightened. It was rumored that IOC members from Africa would support Toronto's bid over

Out of the mouth of babes and sucklings hast thou ordained strength because of thine enemies, that thou mightest still the enemy and the avenger.
—Psalms 8:2, The Bible, King James Version

Paris. The Africans made up fifteen of the IOC's 121 voting members.

Toronto's mayor, Mel Lastman, was eager to attract the Games to his city. A man of small build and grand ambitions, Lastman had made a fortune selling appliances and bargain furniture through his Bad Boy brand. It wasn't long before his devil-may-care attitude followed him into office. At sixty-eight, he was the city's most flamboyant cheerleader.

When it was time for the road show to pitch Toronto, Lastman joined the bid committee to add lustre. The team was heading to Mombasa, Kenya, to lobby delegates who were gathering in the East African city for their regional meeting. But something would go terribly wrong.

Lastman, left unattended for a short while during the stopover in Barcelona on June 8, was approached by freelance reporter Chris Atchison. His request for an interview was granted. The mayor began with a favorite topic: his grandiose tourism plans for his city. Then Atchison asked, "So where are you going next?" Lastman responded, "What the hell do I want to go to a place like Mombasa? Snakes just scare the hell out of me. I'm sort of scared about going there, but the wife is really nervous. I just see myself in a pot of boiling water with all these natives dancing around me."

Lastman's remark was so off-topic it didn't make Atchison's copy when he filed his story with the *Toronto Star*. As an afterthought Atchison added the Mombasa quote. Two weeks later, the story went from the *Star's* sports page to front pages everywhere. The world was looking at Toronto, but not in the way its good citizens wanted.

"What a terrible, terrible, terrible thing to say," said spokesperson and former Olympian Bruce Kidd. "The only

Linguistic intelligence (Word Smart) is the capacity to think in words and to use language to express and appreciate complex meaning.
—Howard Gardner, *Frames of Mind: The Theory of Multiple Intelligences*, 1983

thing I can hope is that the good work that thousands of Canadians have done in Africa and the efforts that so many of us have made to assist our friends and colleagues to strengthen programs for sport in Africa will outweigh these terribly inappropriate remarks."

Toronto Star columnist Royson James captured the sentiment of the city: "Breathtakingly stupid," he wrote on June 21. "How can you 'joke' about stuff like that when you know, or should know, that it is hurtful and insulting to so many of your constituents?" The Globe and Mail summed up the collective mood: "The mayor let the city down with the world watching, revealed a breathtaking ignorance of a whole continent and offended the core values of his electorate, who see themselves as citizens of a sophisticated, multicultural city."

The next day, a contrite Lastman was the star attraction at a hastily organized press conference. Flanked by his press spokesman, Jim Warren, the mayor apologized, while sticking like glue to very few words.

Marx Kahende, deputy Kenyan ambassador to the United Nations, said: "I don't know how he was elected but it appears that something has gone very wrong since that time." —Ben Fenton, "Toronto mayor says sorry for 'cannibals' slur," Telegraph, June 23, 2001

REPORTER: *Mayor, do you think your comments hurt Toronto's Olympic bid?*

LASTMAN: *I am truly sorry, and I'm going to say it again, I'm sorry that my comments were inappropriate. And I want to apologize to everyone for my remarks, particularly anyone who was offended by them.*

REPORTER: *But is sorry enough? Should you resign at this point?*

LASTMAN: *I am sorry I made the remarks.*

REPORTER: *What damage do you think you made to the Olympic bid?*

LASTMAN: *I'm sorry I made the remarks. My comments were inappropriate.*

REPORTER: *That's not what I asked.*

LASTMAN: *That's my answer.*

REPORTER: *How much damage have you done to a multicultural city as the mayor?*

LASTMAN: *I am truly sorry.*

REPORTER: *Are you considering resigning?*

LASTMAN: *I am truly sorry that I made those remarks.*

REPORTER: *Are you considering resigning as a result of making those remarks?*

LASTMAN: *I am truly sorry I made those remarks.*

REPORTER: *Are you considering resigning?*

LASTMAN: *I am truly sorry.*

REPORTER: *What else can you add in terms of damage control? What are you guys doing around damage control, about trying to correct?*

LASTMAN: *I am truly sorry I made the remarks. My comments were inappropriate.*

REPORTER: *Are you going to continue to go to Europe and lobby for the bid and stuff within your schedule as planned?*

LASTMAN: *I am very sorry about the remarks.*

REPORTER: *Are you very sorry about the remarks you made?*

(Laughter)

Warren jumped in. "It's not funny," he said. But it was, as the mayor continued to act as if he had stumbled into the wrong news conference.

He was capable of saying anything, anytime ... revealing a world view shaped in equal parts by Tarzan movies and Bugs Bunny cartoons.
—Stephen Brunt, "The tanned time bomb taints city's Olympic bid," *Globe and Mail*, June 22, 2001

REPORTER: *In all due respect, there are people in the city who are from Kenya; there are people of African descent in the city. Just to be sorry does not explain why you did this. Why did you make this comment?*

LASTMAN: *I am sorry I made the remarks and my comments*

were completely inappropriate. And I want to apologize to anybody who was offended by them.

REPORTER: *Mayor Lastman, did you have a head-slapping moment when you thought you shouldn't have said that?*

LASTMAN: *It was just the wrong thing to say, and I am sorry I made them. I mean what do you want from me, except I'm sorry? I've apologized. I did the wrong thing.*

REPORTER: *Did you goof? You made a mistake.*

LASTMAN: *Of course I did. That's why I'm apologizing.*

REPORTER: *I think what a multicultural city like Toronto wants to know is why you made it in the first place.*

And so it continued. After saying "I'm sorry" twenty times, the mayor, usually bubbling with so much to say grew silent. But he didn't resign.

On July 13, thousands of people gathered in Toronto's Union Station to hear the IOC decision carried live from Moscow on massive television screens. When it was announced that the 2008 Olympic Games were awarded to Beijing, a collective groan muted the city traffic. Toronto's investment in a fleeting chance at international sports glory had failed.

Why did the mayor make the comments in the first place? That was the question. But it's doubtful that Lastman himself knew the answer. He was a man unaware of the mental process that had turned his thoughts into words.

Language most shows a man: Speak, that I may see thee. It springs out of the most retired and inmost parts of us, and is the image of the parent of it, the mind. No glass renders a man's form or likeness so true as his speech.
—Ben Jonson, *Timber, Or Discoveries Made upon Men and Matter*, 1640

Mastering Rule 10

Remember, the quality of what you think informs everything you say, especially in the give-and-take of an interview. Reckless thinking leads to reckless talk. Cultivate the editor in your head by listening to what's being heard. Unfortunately for Mayor Lastman, his stream-of-consciousness rant wound up in print.

Edit your thoughts as they are being formulated into words. Athletes and musicians have learned to anticipate their next moves. Jazz great Oscar Peterson described the process on National Public Radio when explaining the art of improvisation on the piano. He said, "You don't have to have a huge vocabulary to make yourself understood. Because the more that you can use the important words, the better understood you will be. ... You should gain this command of the instrument so you can evaluate the upcoming idea while you are playing the one that is taking place, which you have to do in jazz. You have to think ahead."

Steven Pinker, author of *The Language Instinct*, explains why "thinking ahead" isn't easy for everyone. "In speech, all the steps in the sentence-composition process must be done in real time—one word comes out after another, fractions of seconds apart. One cannot pause for seven seconds before choosing the verb, or go back and 'erase' a word and replace it with a better one while the listener is twiddling her thumbs. In writing, one has the luxury of composing and editing at one's leisure and presenting the world with

Stream of Consciousness: the unedited chronological flow of conscious experience through the mind.
—*Merriam-Webster's Collegiate Dictionary,* 11th Edition

Wayne Gretzky had a "rink sense" that allowed him to play at a level that was far above other players. He could not only envision the whole rink in his mind and how players were moving within it, he could anticipate where the play was going two to three seconds before it happened.
—Jessica Morrison, *Wayne Gretzky: Greatness on Ice,* 2010

the final product." Articulate people have the ability to talk and edit themselves *in real time.*

Life is about editing; use the red pencil in all things. From decorating to speaking, "less is more." Avoid useless phrases and clichés such as "I am of the opinion that" (I believe); "during the course of" (during); "due to the fact that" (because); "at this moment in time" (now); "with all due respect" (I disagree). Also, avoid verbal hedges such as "kind of," "sort of," and the time wasters "uh," "um," "let's see," "you know," and so on.

"Less is more" first appeared in the poem "Andrea del Sarto," written by Robert Browning in 1855. The phrase was popularized by architect Ludwig Mies van der Rohe, who defined modernism as simplicity of style.

Learn to hear yourself as others do. Use a recording device rather than a notebook at meetings and other interactive situations. Do so openly. Listen carefully. What's your verbal signature? Are you repetitive? Do your phrases lack coherence? Are they truncated (you've ended before completing the thought) or loquacious (you're still talking after your colleagues have moved on)? The less time you take to make a point, the more people pay attention.

Remember, leaders must be good communicators. It's the one job that can't be outsourced or delegated. Specifically, leaders must frame and manage meaning. In his 1978 essay "Leadership Is a Language Game," Louis R. Pondy explains, "This dual capacity to make sense of things and to put them into language meaningful to a large number of people gives the person who has it enormous leverage." Pondy cites an iconic example: "The real power of Martin Luther King, Jr., was not only that he had a dream but that he could describe it, that it became public, and therefore accessible to millions of people."

Communication Leadership

When Lee Iacocca was chief executive officer of the Chrysler Corporation, he treated reporters like clients. In 1980, Iacocca lobbied for a highly controversial federal loan guarantee of $1.2 billion and saved Chrysler from bankruptcy. In his words, "There were times in our dark days at Chrysler when we had no weapons left in our arsenal except our ability to communicate." Iacocca pioneered the era of the CEO as media pitchman and brand champion. It was Iacocca who popularized the phrase "the level playing field." That was the metaphor he used in selling Chrysler's story to the media. The loan, he argued, would allow Chrysler to compete with Japanese automakers.

Don't call on the media if you are not prepared to answer questions. Lastman showed up, then refused to give an account of himself. As mayor, he could have used the opportunity to contrast, for example, his hurtful remarks with the city's long-standing commitment to diversity. That would have been a fitting apology. Instead, Lastman trivialized the words "I'm sorry" with his endless repetitions.

Combative or sarcastic personalities will sound that way if they haven't learned to hear themselves. On March 24, 1989, the Exxon Valdez ran aground as it moved through Prince William Sound, Alaska, causing a massive environmental disaster. Exxon's chief executive officer, Lawrence G. Rawl, received a failing grade from audiences for his flippant comments in news reports and his tardy arrival to the scene.

Time's Richard Behar caught up with Rawl a year later. He asked, "Exxon was charged with 'arrogance.' Are you arrogant?" Rawl's response was a shocker. He said, "We would have liked to recall the oil off the Prince William Sound. We called but it didn't hear us." The story appeared in the March 26, 1990 issue of *Time* magazine under the headline "Exxon Strikes Back."

In 2005, the February 15 edition of *Forbes* magazine reported briefly on Rawl's death. It had been fifteen years since the spill, yet the story included a quote from William K. Reilly, former head of the U.S. Environmental Protection Agency. "Rawl," he said, "provided a casebook example of how not to communicate to the public when your company messes up."

Tactic

Knowing the vocabulary you tend to favor in conversations is an important step toward acing an on-the-record interview. Once you have identified these words, make sure they mean what you think they mean and that you are using them correctly. Eliminate or substitute any word you mispronounce or trip over more than once. When speaking in public, don't reach for words that are unfamiliar or words you're not sure how to pronounce. Explore the dictionary and build your vocabulary at home.

Game Face Conduct

Thoughts become words. Even those blessed with verbal intelligence sometimes say the wrong thing. But harmful remarks that betray prejudices, beliefs and intentions are more serious than a misspoken word. Gaffes are glitches in the verbal process; the other speaks to character. After all, the editor in your head can only flag what it *knows* to be wrong.

And Finally

Don't engage a heckler unless you know exactly how it's going to turn out. They can be more lethal than reporters. Governor Mitt Romney learned this lesson during the 2011 Republican presidential primary season. He was appearing before a mostly friendly crowd at the Iowa State Fair. Romney was expressing his opposition to raising taxes when a protestor shouted, "Corporations!" The speaker was urging Romney to raise taxes on companies that benefit from loopholes in the tax code. Romney responded, "Corporations are people, my friend." Some in the audience laughed. Others chimed in with a "No, they are not." "Of course they are,"

Editors Wanted

What I'm hearing, which is sort of scary, is they all want to stay in Texas. Everyone is so overwhelmed by the hospitality. And so many of the people in the arena here, you know, were underprivileged anyway, so this is working very well for them.
—Former first lady Barbara Bush visiting Hurricane Katrina evacuees housed at the Astrodome, *Marketplace*, American Public Media, September 5, 2005

Considering the dire circumstances that we have in New Orleans, virtually a city that has been destroyed, things are going relatively well.
—Michael Brown, director of Federal Emergency Management Agency, CNN, September 1, 2005

Romney said. "Everything corporations earn go to people; where do you think it goes?" Romney's responses energized a situation that played out on newscasts that evening and, thereafter, to the delight of his political opponents. Hecklers win if they gain attention and throw you off your game.

Here are some "Do's and Don'ts" if confronted: Do address hecklers directly. Tell them they are interrupting an event that the audience came to hear. Invite them to stay and listen or leave. Don't debate or acknowledge any topic they raise. Don't ask the audience who they want to hear, or offer to give up the microphone. Do not continue speaking over the heckler; wait for security or the organizer to intervene. Do show your patience and good humor.

Editors Wanted

As you know, you have to go to war with the army you have, not the army you want or wish to have at a later time.
—Donald Rumsfeld, U.S. defense secretary, at a town hall meeting with U.S. soldiers in Kuwait December 8, 2004

We have been the cowards. Lobbing cruise missiles from 2,000 miles away, that's cowardly. Staying in the airplane when it hits the building, say what you want about it, that's not cowardly.
—Host Bill Maher, talking about U.S. military bombers over Iraq in contrast to actions of 9/11 hijackers, *Politically Incorrect*, September 17, 2001

Respond Even If You Can't Answer

Never say "No comment," regardless of how tough or
tactless the question. That said, there are questions for
which there are no right answers. Still you must respond.
Joan of Arc faced months of intense probing at her trial.
The questions were intended to trap and expose her as
a witch and heretic, but somehow Joan knew to respond
without answering. When asked *the* question designed to
discredit her claim that she was being guided by God, hers
was a deliberately artful reply.

The Maid of Orleans

If I am not, may God place me there. If I am, may God so
keep me.
—Joan of Arc

In 1426, during the Late Middle Ages, a thirteen-year-old
Catholic girl saw a vision while sitting in the yard of her father's farm. As she explained years later, she was frightened
but calmed herself when she realized it was the voice of
Saint Michael sent to her from the King of Heaven. The angel prepared Joan for visits from Saint Catherine and Saint
Margaret bearing messages. By the time she was nineteen,
inspired and guided by her angels, Joan of Arc would march
into battle and into legend.

Joan lived with her family in Domrémy in northwest
France. Though small and remote, the village was well traf-
ficked with soldiers since France was at war—and had been
for ages. The Hundred Years War was a long and bloody conflict started in 1337 by the English King Edward III, who, as
the grandson of a French king, claimed the right to also rule
France. The English already controlled northern France and,
after a decisive victory at the Battle of Agincourt in 1415, the
country was more divided than ever.

The French king, Charles VI, suffered bouts of madness,
which fanned the ambitions of feuding princes; his uncle
Philip, Duke of Burgundy, was allied with the English while
his brother Louis, Duke of Orleans, wanted to drive the

She had no means of
knowing where the
interrogation is driving,
where the concealed
charge is.
—Marina Warner, *Joan of*
Arc: The Image of Female
Heroism, University of
California Press, 1981

English out. Over the decades the whole country, including the clergy, fell into rival factions of pro-English Burgundians and pro-French Armagnacs. The king's only surviving son and heir, the dauphin [Charles VII], was disinherited under the Treaty of Troyes. With his own mother in the English camp, it would take a miracle to unite France and restore the dauphin's kingdom.

Against this canvas of war and civil strife, Joan spent her days tending the animals, weaving, and spinning when not in prayer. Domrémy was in a region that recognized the authority of the Duke of Burgundy, but the town remained loyal to the dauphin. By her own account, when she was about seventeen, "Two or three times a week this Voice exhorted me to go to France. My father knew nothing of my going. The Voice kept urging me; I could no longer endure it. It told me I would raise the siege of Orleans." Located on the Loire River in north-central France, Orleans was the last French stronghold in the region. For six months, allied English and Burgundian forces had been bombarding the village from siege points around the heavily fortified walls. The inhabitants would have to surrender or risk starvation if they were not rescued.

In February 1429, Joan took to the road searching for a military escort to take her to the dauphin. Her mission was to expel the English and see him crowned. She was rebuffed by the regional commander, but weeks later he relented. When Joan reached the court at Chinon, she was granted an audience with the dauphin. Then Joan was sent to Poitiers to be tested by theologians before permission was granted. Such was the desperation of the would-be ruler that the teenage girl was given a horse and special armor, and allowed to lead his army.

In May, ten days after her dramatic arrival at Orleans, the siege was lifted. Joan's sudden appearance at the battle was seen as the fulfillment of an ancient prophecy that France would be liberated by a maiden. A month later, the French won a great victory at Patay and drove the English out of the Loire Valley. In 1430, after a chain of victories, Joan was captured and ransomed to the English for 10,000 francs. Joan's military career lasted one year. During that brief period, she had drawn the curtain on the final act of the Hundred Years War.

> A holy prophetess new risen up,
> Is come with a great power to raise the siege.
> —William Shakespeare, Henry VI, Act 1, Scene 4

Joan was taken to Rouen, the seat of the English provisional government. She was chained and shackled and placed in the tower with guards posted inside and outside her cell. Pierre Cauchon, the bishop of Beauvais and a staunch English partisan, made arrangements for Joan to be tried in an ecclesiastic court. She was charged with heresy and witchcraft, crimes punishable by death. Joan was denied counsel and the right to call witnesses. Joan's voices, however, would guide her.

In February 1431, Joan appeared before sixty-two clerics for the infamous show trial. She took the oath after first declaring, "You may ask me such things as I will not tell you ... for you may constrain me to say things that I have sworn not to say; then I should be perjured, which you ought not to wish."

Cauchon's friend and ally, cleric Jean Beaupère, relished his role as chief prosecutor and tormentor.

BEAUPÈRE: *The last two occasions on which you have heard this Voice, did a light come?*

JOAN OF ARC: *The light comes at the same time as the Voice.*

BEAUPÈRE: *Besides the Voice, do you see anything?*

JOAN OF ARC: *I will not tell you all: I have not leave; my oath does not touch on that. My Voice is good and to be honored. I am not bound to answer you about it. I request that the points on which I do not now answer may be given me in writing.*

BEAUPÈRE: *The Voice from whom you ask counsel, has it a face and eyes?*

JOAN OF ARC: *You shall not know yet. There is a saying among children, that sometimes one is hanged for speaking the truth.*

BEAUPÈRE: *Do you know if you are in the grace of God?*

JOAN OF ARC: *If I am not, may God place me there; if I am, may God so keep me. I shall be the saddest creature in all of the world if I knew that I were not in the grace of God.*

Joan's reply "stupefied" her interrogators according to one of the notaries present. To presume to be in God's grace was to commit heresy. But for Joan to deny her voices was to deny God. It was a catch-22. In 1896, her biographer, Mark Twain, said of Joan's performance: "Untaught wisdom which overmatched their learning, battled their tricks and treacheries with native sagacity which compelled wonder, and scored every day a victory against incredible odds."

Sometimes there was humor.

ASSESSOR: *Does not Saint Margaret speak English?*

JOAN OF ARC: *Why should she speak English, when she is not on the English side?*

Mostly, Joan deflected questions intended to expose her as cunning or vain.

Once when Joan was questioned by someone whether she was in a state of grace, and I had said that this was a grave question, and that Joan was not bound to answer such a question, the Bishop of Beauvaus said to me, "It would be better for you if you had kept your mouth shut."
—Professor Jean Lefèvre, Assessor, Joan's Nullification trial, 1452

A "catch-22" [Joseph Heller] is a problematic situation for which the only solution is denied by circumstances inherent in the problem or by a rule.
—Merriam-Webster's Collegiate Dictionary, 11th Edition

ASSESSOR: *Do you know that the people of your party had services, masses, and prayer offered for you?*

JOAN OF ARC: *I know nothing of it; if they had any service, it was not by my order; but if they prayed for me, my opinion is they did not do ill.*

ASSESSOR: *Did those of your party firmly believe that you were sent from God?*

JOAN OF ARC: *I do not know if they believed it, and in this I refer to their own feelings in this matter.*

Embarrassed by her deft replies, the interrogators terminated the public hearing after the sixth session. Cauchon ordered the trial to continue in Joan's cell with fewer inquisitors. But the notaries would capture her eloquence, enabling Twain to observe four centuries later, "[A]nd when insultingly asked why it was that her standard had place at the crowning of the king in the Cathedral of Rheims rather than the standards of the other captains, she uttered that touching speech, 'It had borne the burden, it had earned the honor.'" George Bernard Shaw was so taken with Joan's words that he used them verbatim in his 1923 play, *Saint Joan*.

What the clerics needed was a new tactic for the inevitable ending. And they had one. Dressing in male attire was forbidden under canon law and Joan could hardly deny that she dressed so on the battlefield.

BEAUPÈRE: *Was it God who prescribed to you the dress of a man?*

JOAN OF ARC: *What concerns this dress is a small thing—less than nothing. I did not take it by evidence of any man in the world. I did not take this dress to do anything but by the command of our Lord and the Angels.*

I know for certain that Joan had no director, counselor, or defender to the end of the trial, and that no one would have dared apply themselves to counseling, directing, or defending her, from fear of the English.
—Friar Martin Ladvenu, Assessor, May 9, 1452

BEAUPÈRE: *Did it appear to you that this command to take man's dress was lawful?*
JOAN OF ARC: *All I have done is by Our Lord's command. If I had been told to take some other, I should have done it: because it would have been His command.*

Beaupère chose to ignore the practical need for Joan's attire on the battlefield.

BEAUPÈRE: *In this particular case, this taking of man's dress, do you think you did well?*
JOAN OF ARC: *I have done nothing in the world but by the order of God.*

In 1853, Charles Dickens wrote of her ordeal, "how they had Jeanne [Joan] out to examine her, and cross-examine her, and re-examine her, and worry her into saying anything and everything."

Joan was found guilty of cross dressing, declared a lapsed heretic, and excommunicated. After the church was done with her, Cauchon handed her back to the English commanders for punishment. Joan was burned at the stake in the churchyard of St. Ouen on May 24, 1431. Twenty years later, her trial was nullified and the church declared Joan a martyr. Over the centuries she has become an enduring symbol of French nationalism.

Joan of Arc has been the subject of countless films, plays, and books. Yet the transcript of her trial remains her true testament. Joan's inspired responses to trick questions make it possible to believe that a simple farmer's daughter could have been divinely inspired to lead armies, win battles, and give wise counsel to kings.

These later biographers see the examiners' tendency to ask questions whose connection to each other Joan likewise could not grasp as even stronger evidence of their nefarious intentions.
—Karen Sullivan, *The Interrogation of Joan of Arc*, University of Minnesota Press, 1999

Mastering Rule 11

Never say "No comment" when asked a question. It's the refuge of criminals, scoundrels, and others with something to hide.

Always respond, even when you cannot answer. In the dictionary, "respond" and "answer" are used interchangeably, but in interviews they are more aligned to their etymological meaning of reply (to re-spond) versus swear (to an-swer). To respond is to acknowledge the question, whereas to answer is to satisfy the question.

BUSINESSWEEK: What's a fair evaluation [of Amazon's stock]?
BEZOS: I've never taken a position on stock price, and I don't think it's appropriate for management to take a position on the stock price. [Management's] job is to build an important, lasting, valuable company, and to work hard at that.
—Jeff Bezos, "Chewing Sashimi with Jeff Bezos," *BusinessWeek*, July 14, 2002

Beware of the "set-up" question. This question is being asked to frame the question to come. It may not sound ominous in itself. In the case of Joan of Arc, the English were desperate to discredit all belief that Joan's mission was divine. At one point Beaupère asked Joan if she'd been fasting, then immediately asked her when she last heard the voices. His aim was to place into evidence the likelihood that Joan's visions were hallucinations brought on by her impairment from hunger.

Don't let inquisitors put words into your mouth. Be polite but forceful on this point. Do not repeat language or phrases used in questions unless they match your sentiments, exactly.

Avoid invitations to delve into the motivations of others. It's rarely in your interest to do so. Such questions are often designed to lead you into conflict with competitors, supervisors, colleagues, and so on. All are bound to be offended by your guesswork or characterizations. For example, Joan is asked over and over to speculate on the thoughts of others and to speak about her audience with Charles VII, which she resisted repeatedly.

Speak as if your words will appear exactly as spoken. It does not matter if your statements will be published verbatim or paraphrased into a narrative, as is normally the case in media reports. Verbatim transcripts are standard at trials or formal hearings where the outcome will have consequences. While interviews are not usually a matter of life and death, interview subjects should respect each word spoken.

Tactic

There are times when it is appropriate to respond to a question with a question. This is especially true when questions are asked with malevolence. Joan used the tactic throughout her trial. For example:

CLERIC: *Do you know by revelation if you will escape?*

JOAN: *Do you wish me to speak against myself?*

CLERIC: *Why did you not enter Lacharite, if you had command from God to do so?*

JOAN: *Who told you I had command from God?*

CLERIC: *Have your Angels never failed you in the good things of Grace?*

JOAN: *How can he fail me, when he comforts me every day?*

FROST: Do you quite like him [Harold Wilson]?
HEATH: Well I think in politics you see, it's not a question of going about liking people or not. It's a question of dealing with people. I've always been able to deal perfectly well with Minister Wilson, as indeed he has with me.
FROST: But do you like him?
HEATH: Well again, it's not a question of likes or dislikes. It's a question of working together with other people who are in politics.
FROST: But do you like him?
HEATH: That'll have to remain to be seen, won't it?
—David Frost with British Prime Minister Edward Heath, *BBC Omnibus*, 1974

Game Face Conduct

Don't be defensive if you don't know the answer or don't wish to answer a question outside your area of expertise. In this predicament Joan responded with, "Of this I know nothing, nor have I ever heard of it." There will be times when it is appropriate to say you will provide the information at a later date. When Joan wished to ponder a question, she remarked, "Tomorrow, I will answer on it." A wise person knows what they should know and what they are not required to know.

And Finally

Joan of Arc may have invented the "push-button response," but President Bill Clinton was the master practitioner during the scandal that led to his impeachment by the House of Representatives in 1998. The push-button response is a boiler-plate phrase intended to shut down a line of inquiry with a positive message that can be repeated. It's the stop button for conversations the speaker chooses not to have. The push-button response is best utilized in a crisis.

Joan's inquisitors were determined to find contradictions that would place her at odds with church, king, and God. When asked if she believed herself subject to the pope and bishops, Joan responded, "I believe myself to be subject to them, but God must be served first." "God must be first" was Joan's push-button response, a verbal code to her clerics that her angels trumped their earthly authority.

Clinton, who faced a year-long barrage of questions about Monica Lewinsky, crafted his stock phrase to remind everyone that he was still working hard, and still the president of the United States. (It was Clinton who coined the phrase "the politics of personal destruction.")

SOLOMON: I assume your salary is well above a million dollars.
DOBBS: I'm well compensated but underpaid.
SOLOMON: More like a million?
DOBBS: If I answer that, do we keep going until we arrive at the precise figure?
—Lou Dobbs with Deborah Solomon, *New York Times Magazine*, March 21, 2004

On January 21, 1998, when the story was breaking, the president responded, *"I think that is all I should say right now so I can get back to the work of the country."*

On January 27, 1998, Clinton ended the initial denial with, *"These allegations are false. And I need to go back to work for the American people."*

On September 2 1998, Clinton said, *"I am going back to work. I believe that's what the American people want me to do ... and that's what I intend to do."*

On January 13, 1999, Clinton said, *"And I think in the meantime I need to work on the business of the people."*

Clinton's push-button response was effective. He had asked Americans to stick by him as he voiced his commitment to focus on his job; and in poll after poll the majority stayed with him.

Never Repeat "Negative" Language

Most of the embarrassing sound bites that make their way into the media come out of the mouths of the interviewees themselves. It's natural for reporters to phrase questions using "negative" or provocative language to make a point, but these phrases only stick when repeated by the subjects themselves. Queen Elizabeth's daughter-in-law Sophie Rhys-Jones once answered a highly indelicate question with the perfect tabloid headline.

My Edward Is Not Gay

I can tell you he's not gay. I had heard something before we met, but I put it down to the fact that he was working in theatre and people had presumed he was gay.
—Sophie Rhys-Jones, Countess of Wessex

On March 14, 2001, the Countess of Wessex, Sophie Rhys-Jones, arrived at London's posh Dorchester Hotel for a luncheon meeting in a £12,000-per-day suite. Already in attendance was Murray Harkin, her business partner at R-JH, their public relations firm. Harkin introduced Rhys-Jones to a prospective client—Sheik Mohammed and the sheik's assistant. Harkin had met with the sheik on two previous occasions to pitch the firm's services. Now the PR duo was hoping an appearance by Rhys-Jones would secure a £20,000-per-month contract to promote the sheik's leisure complex in Dubai.

How I'd love to be able to go out and sing from the rooftops: it is not true. I want to prove it to people, but it's impossible to do that.
—Sophie Rhys-Jones, Countess of Wessex, *News of the World*, April 1, 2001

Rhys-Jones was the picture of decorum, as one would expect of the wife of Prince Edward, the Queen of England's youngest son. The countess made sure to counsel the sheik that he should not expect special treatment because of her royal attachments. But soon her conversation suggested otherwise. Rhys-Jones began gossiping about family members and high-ranking politicians.

She started with Prime Minister Tony Blair, referring to him pejoratively as "President Blair" while describing his wife Cherie, a lawyer, as "horrid."

RHYS-JONES: *He's ignorant of the countryside. His wife is even worse; she hates the countryside. She hates it! And because the popular vote is within the city, he's going to go with that all the time.*

SHEIK'S ASSISTANT: *She [Cherie] seems low key.*

RHYS-JONES: *She's an intelligent woman and I think she wanted to keep her hand in. Or maybe she didn't think her husband's government was going to last long so she'd have to go back to work anyway.*

When asked who would be on the losing side after the next election, Rhys-Jones fingered William Hague, the Conservative leader of the opposition, who she described as "deformed."

RHYS-JONES: *It's a shame really because William is very intelligent. I think he's got real vision. But he's got this awful kind of way he talks, like that all the time [mimicking Hague's Yorkshire accent]. He sounds like a puppet unfortunately.*

Former Conservative Prime Minister John Major was next. Rhys-Jones described Margaret Thatcher's successor as "completely wooden," and alleged that he "used the royals to cover up a lot of things they [his government] were doing." Then Rhys-Jones turned to the recent budget by chancellor of the exchequer and future prime minister, Gordon Brown.

RHYS-JONES: *It's a load of pap. ... What they failed to say is that the figure of increase in everybody's taxes is something frightening since the Labour party came to power; the man in the street is paying something like an additional 40 percent in taxes.*

The discussion moved to possible celebrity endorsements for the Dubai venture when the countess made a comparison between herself and the late Diana, Princess of Wales.

RHYS-JONES: *Everyone said, "Gosh, doesn't she look like Diana?" Then they thought, "This isn't going to be much good because she's not going to be turning up every day in different outfits, opening children's hospitals," you know. I do some of that but not as much as they'd like.*

And if the countess hadn't said enough, she tossed off the assessment that her brother-in-law Prince Charles and his companion Camilla Parker Bowles were "possibly number one on people's unpopular people list." For the sheik and his assistant, it had been a most memorable day.

After the luncheon, Rhys-Jones went to R-JH's office in fashionable Mayfair. Within a short time, she became aware that the meeting she had just attended was a sham orchestrated by the Rupert Murdoch–owned *News of the World*. The Sunday tabloid was known for its obsessive, celebrity-studded coverage. The robe-clad sheik was a photojournalist, and the man posing as his assistant was actually Mazher Mahmood, the *News of the World's* notorious investigative reporter.

Mahmood was famous for his signature disguises used to fool interview subjects. Harkin had been the original sting target. Rhys-Jones and Harkin were subjects of a loud whispering campaign that alleged the pair used her royal connection to drum up business. To the delight of the tabloid editors, the investigation of Harkin had ensnared a member of the royal family. According to news reports, the only inquiry R-JH made in advance of the meeting was a request to

But it is a technique that should surely be used sparingly because it can too easily be abused. There is a fine line between the use of subterfuge and the act of entrapment.
—Roy Greenslade, "Why I'm out to nail Mazher Mahmood," *Independent*, April 15, 2006

see the Dorchester luncheon menu.

Rhys-Jones was further dismayed to discover Mahmood had secretly recorded the conversation. Her distress would deepen when she learned that, during Harkin's initial meeting with Mahmood, the men had broached the topic of her husband's sexual orientation. Speculation had swirled in the late eighties, around the time the prince worked with Andrew Lloyd Webber's Really Useful Theatre Company (by 1990, the buzz was enough to make the royal bachelor publicly denounce the rumors as being "so unfair to me and my family. I am not gay"). Mahmood had also taped his initial meetings with Harkin, who allegedly could be heard saying of the rumors, "I'm a great believer that there's no smoke without fire."

Sensing disaster, Rhys-Jones alerted Buckingham Palace. Lawyers representing R-JH swung into action. They obtained a court injunction against *News of the World*. A judge ordered the tabloid to turn over its tapes and transcripts. On March 21, seven days after the sting operation, the Palace's communications director, Simon Walker, approached *News of the World*'s editor Rebekah Wade (known as Rebekah Brooks after her 2009 marriage). The two were reported to have struck a deal: the newspaper would not publish the sting conversations in exchange for an "exclusive interview" with the countess. The Palace would get copy approval before publication. Members of the newspaper staff grumbled. They worried that a so-called exclusive interview with Rhys-Jones would not provide a story half as juicy as the one they already had. To their delight, they would be proven wrong.

The next day on March 22, 2001, Rhys-Jones sat down with *News of the World*'s reporter Carole Aye Maung in the Regency drawing room at Buckingham Palace. The countess answered questions about her fertility, her experiences

"Media bias" is the tendency of reporters and editors to approach an event with a preconceived point of view or prejudice, leading to coverage that is unfair, one-sided, or framed to fit an agenda. Whereas, objectivity is the hallmark of journalism.

We use subterfuge because we have to, and do so in the public interest, sometimes at great personal risk to the journalists involved. Police officers employ similar methods.
—Andy Coulson, "We can do without lessons in ethics from Roy Greenslade," *Independent*, April 22, 2006

dealing with the tabloid press, and rumors of a mock marriage with Prince Edward, her husband of two years. "I mean, you know, supposedly separate bedrooms. That's a load of rubbish," responded the countess, adding, "supposedly living apart all week. We are probably apart maybe one, maybe two nights a week. Which is a lot less than an awful lot of other people. I really don't think I could be part of a marriage that was a complete sham." When asked about her husband's sexual preference, she replied, "I can tell you he's not gay. I had heard something before we met, but I put it down to the fact that he was working in theatre and people had presumed he was gay." For Rhys-Jones, things had gone from bad to worse!

The morning of Sunday, April 1, the tabloid's headline read: "Sophie: My Edward is Not Gay." *News of the World's* rival, the *Mail on Sunday,* went with a headline that shouted, "Queen's Outrage at Sophie Insults." R-JH was a rolling PR disaster.

One week after publishing its exclusive with her, *News of the World* reneged on its agreement with the Palace and printed transcripts of the sting tapes. Various versions of the caper were now in the hands of rival newspapers. Few believed *News of the World's* claim that it published the full transcript in order to exonerate Rhys-Jones because of "gross inaccuracies" being printed elsewhere.

The media had a field day. Rhys-Jones was criticized up and down Fleet Street for her indiscretions. Kate Nicolas, an editor of *PRWeek,* questioned why Rhys-Jones spoke as she did at what was supposed to be a business meeting. "She has broken her own ground rules," said Nicolas. Her participation in the make-up interview was seen as PR blunder number two. As Derek Brown of the *Guardian* put it, she

The head of press at Buckingham Palace came in for a whole other flap because this was thought to be such a ridiculous deal and as you say, the headline did not work in Sophie's favor; it did not work in the royal family's favor.
—Cathy Newman, *Reliable Sources,* CNN, April 15, 2001

"blurted out further and more personal indiscretions about her marriage." Others found it ironic that Rhys-Jones could err so easily on two separate occasions. But some had no such qualms, implying R-JH was not a serious outfit.

Of her many indiscretions, the worst by far were Rhys-Jones' statements on government leaders. Members of the British royal family are never to comment on politics. On April 9, amid the furor of bad press, an embattled Rhys-Jones announced she was resigning from her position at R-JH. The agency never regained its footing and suffered heavy financial losses.

Five years later, in 2006, the R-JH agency closed its doors for good. In 2011, the *News of the World* newspaper was shut down by Rupert and his son James Murdoch after the notorious phone hacking scandal and allegations of an unscrupulous newsroom.

Rhys-Jones paid dearly for her mistakes but she received little sympathy. She discussed subjects best avoided and embellished rather than kept to the inside lane of probing questions. By repeating negatives, she gave new life to old tales.

While condemning tabloid journalism, broadsheets steal our stories and fill column inches with details of our exposés for their own readers.
—Mazher Mahmood, *Confessions of a Fake Sheik*, 2008

Mastering Rule 12

I am deeply distressed
by the carrying out of an
entrapment operation on
me and my business but I
also much regret my own
misjudgment in succumbing
to that subterfuge.
—Sophie Rhys-Jones,
Countess of Wessex,
statement, April 8, 2001

Avoid drinking with reporters. Even though the sheik was a fake, the meeting was a trap, and the conversation was secretly recorded, all the blame fell to Rhys-Jones because of her indiscretions.

Do not get into the habit of repeating the question. By doing so, you will appear to be stalling or buying time. Second and most important, questions usually have loaded or negative words which the interview subject takes ownership of when repeated. Rhys-Jones should have answered the question without using the word "gay," which made the headline possible. While the word "gay" is not a negative word, it held a negative connotation in this context, given the prince's public denial years before. When asked, Rhys-Jones should have replied, "My husband and I enjoy normal marital relations," or some such bland response.

Don't be afraid of the one-word answer. There are times when "yes" or "no" will do. During the Senate confirmation hearing in 2006, Supreme Court nominee Samuel Alito was grilled by Democrats about his links to an organization that allegedly discriminated against women and minorities. To counter the accusation, Republican Senator Lindsey Graham threw him a gift question, "Are you really a closet bigot?" Alito replied, "I'm not any kind of bigot, I'm not." It was a good-enough answer, but it struck some as funny and became a comedic punch line. Alito should have simply replied, "No," or "No, I'm not." When rebutting a negative, don't repeat the negative.

Unless it is in your interest to do so—and it rarely is—do not embellish your answers. Rhys-Jones never seemed to know when she had addressed the question. She provided distracting details in her overly generous replies. It was no doubt unwelcome news to many that sexual orientation is a precursor for a career in the theatre. As for married couples, they now had a royal standard for what was "normal" in terms of nights spent apart. And Rhys-Jones confirmed, without being asked, the fact that rumors about her husband were so widespread that she had heard them years before.

Don't assume the interview is going well because it is running long. The more focused your narrative, the less time a reporter needs to spend with you. Most journalists can recognize a good quote or sound bite the second they hear one. If the interview drags on, it's probably because you've strayed from your agenda or lost track of your storyline. The more extraneous the content, the more editing you leave to the reporter—the more you fragment your messages.

Tactic

Pauses add tempo and rhythm to the spoken word, and suggest that what is being said is important. Interviews can be stressful and so there is a tendency for novice newsmakers to rush through them. Five or ten seconds can seem like an eternity, but it may be just the moment you need to take a breath to collect yourself. Some interviewers will deliberately pause to see what an anxious subject may say to fill

There are times when we cross the line, but the overriding factor is the public interest, I think. I have never been prosecuted.
—Mazher Mahmood giving evidence at The Leveson Inquiry: Culture, Practice, and Ethics of the Press, December 12, 2011

Public Interest includes, but is not confined to
i) detecting or exposing crime or serious impropriety;
ii) protecting public health and safety;
iii) preventing the public from being misled by an action or statement of an individual or organisation.
—"The Code of Practice," the Press Complaints Commission, 1991

On Thursday July 7, 2011, News Corporation announced that it was shutting down the *News of the World*. The 168-year-old tabloid was at the center of a scandal after it was revealed that staff at the paper routinely hacked into the voice messages of celebrities and crime victims to get scoops.

In October 2013, eight people pleaded not guilty at the start of what British commentators were calling the "Trial of the Century." The defendants included Andy Coulson and Rebekah Brooks, two of Rupert Murdoch's most trusted news executives. The "phone hacking" trial lasted eight months. Brooks was acquitted. Coulson was found guilty and sentenced to 18 months in prison.

In 2016, the fake sheikh, Mazher Mahmood, was charged with tampering with evidence following one of his sting operations and sentenced to 15 months in jail.

the void. Be comfortable with silence. It's a hallmark of confidence. During periods of silence you may even hear the speaker's intentions.

Game Face Conduct

Gossip is hurtful to those being trivialized and reflects poorly on the speaker. It's the height of folly if done during an interview. The fact that Rhys-Jones wrote speedy apologies to the politicians she had talked about was proof that these comments were better left unsaid. If you don't wish to embarrass yourself as the source, don't speak disparagingly of others.

And Finally

Unlike interviewers, playwrights and screenwriters can be counted on to put the right words in people's mouths. Their characters are articulate, and when they are not, it's intentional. The defining moments are there for dramatic effect. In fiction and in real life, people reveal themselves through the spoken word. In his book, *The Playwright's Guidebook: An insightful primer on the art of dramatic writing*, Stuart Spencer poses the question: "After all, what else is there to playwriting except writing dialogue?" According to Spencer, it's "the one, solitary means by which you have to express everything you have to say: theme, character, story, plot. Everything." And he concludes with what sounds like advice for interview subjects: "There is not much to say, in my opinion, about how dramatic language works, except for the following, which is crucial: the words you choose, and the order in which they are delivered, will determine what people think of your play."

RULE 13

Don't Be Seduced by the Attention

Interviews can be as seductive as sex. It is oh-so flattering
to see your words set off in quotes and to be courted
by star reporters. A sudden rush of media attention
has caused many to abandon their true selves and best
judgment. In the Microsoft antitrust case, the trial judge's
reputation was left in tatters. Judge Thomas Penfield
Jackson was publicly rebuked for "pandering to the press"
and indulging in the "American passion for publicity." How
could this have happened?

A Passion for Publicity

[Bill Gates] has a Napoleonic concept of himself and his company, an arrogance that derives from power and unalloyed success, with no leavening hard experiences, no reverses.
—Judge Thomas Penfield Jackson

Thomas Penfield Jackson had been a district circuit judge for sixteen years when he was named to preside over one of the most important antitrust trials in U.S. history: The United States v. Microsoft Corporation. The company, founded by Bill Gates, was making billions churning out its Windows operating system for personal computers. Watching Microsoft's growth keenly was the Justice Department's Antitrust Division. Attorneys there had long maintained that something was foul in the software giant's marketing practices, and after eight years of legal skirmishes, the government was ready to bring Microsoft to trial.

On May 18, 1998, the Justice Department and twenty states filed suit against Microsoft. They charged the company with abusing its market dominance at the expense of rivals such as Intel Corporation, Sun Microsystems, and Netscape Corporation. With a 90 percent market share, Microsoft continued to aggressively bundle its Internet Explorer browser with its operating system, effectively shutting out competitors in an industry worth $40 billion in annual revenues. Government lawyers described the

It is meant that noble minds ever to their likes; for who is so firm that cannot be seduced.
—William Shakespeare, *Julius Caesar*, Act 1, Scene 3

practice as a direct attack on Netscape and argued it was a violation of a 1995 legal decree.

As news of the high-tech battle moved to the front pages, all eyes turned toward Judge Jackson. A former navy officer and a Harvard Law School graduate, Jackson was known to be "fair" and "accommodating" in the courtroom. According to one news source, Jackson was "no technology buff." While he owned a computer, he hardly ever used it. He admired men like Barry Goldwater and John McCain for their independence. Whatever his politics, Jackson wasn't a captive of corporate America. If he was a company man, that company was the U.S. government.

The trial starring the world's richest man began on October 19, 1998. Intent on keeping a tight rein on proceedings, Jackson refused to grant the press any special accreditation. *Time* magazine reported that journalists had to "queue up for hours to sit on a couple of rows of hard benches— first come, first served." Journalists with three of America's leading publications, the *Wall Street Journal*, the *New York Times*, and the *New Yorker* were there for the long haul. They would be rewarded.

The *New Yorker's* Ken Auletta wrote Jackson asking for a meeting. "He invited me to drop by his office," wrote Auletta in *World War 3.0: Microsoft and Its Enemies*, the book he eventually wrote about the case. "I told him that I hoped that later on in the process I might be able to interview him. He was noncommittal. Eventually, Judge Jackson agreed to cooperate for the book."

The trial's witness list was a Who's Who from the tech world's executive roster, including the chief executive officer of Netscape, Jim Barksdale. On November 9, Gates testified in a videotaped deposition from Microsoft's offices in Redmond, Washington. He refuted claims that Microsoft deliberately kept rivals from competing. Elizabeth Wasserman of CNN described his testimony as a "rambling fifty-minute segment pulled from Gates' three-day deposition" where he "engaged in a verbal duel with U.S. Justice Department attorney David Boies, splitting hairs over literal interpretations of e-mails and memos and refusing to concede that company officials focused their efforts primarily on Netscape."

Wasserman relayed how Judge Jackson laughed audibly and shook his head during what she called the sometimes comical war of words in the courtroom. "Jackson hasn't made much effort to hide his impatience with some of Microsoft's bevy of lawyers ...; he has chastised some attorneys in open court and pressured others to step up the pace of their cross-examination."

The trial wrapped up on September 21, 1999, eleven months after it started. The next day Auletta and Jackson met privately in the judge's chambers. Jackson talked about his work and life in a conversation that lasted four hours. Over the next months, there were three on-the-record interviews. Later it would be revealed that the judge agreed to speak about the trial on the condition that his comments remained embargoed until he had rendered his final decision.

By early November, Judge Jackson set the world's media aflutter when he issued his findings of fact, citing that Microsoft held monopoly powers and used them to harm consumers, rivals, and other companies.

On April 3, 2000, two days after mediation efforts failed to bring the sides together, Microsoft shares plunged 40 percent. At the close of trading, Jackson issued his conclusions of law, ruling that Microsoft used predatory methods to

He had a big green book that he took into court every day under his arm. He sat down on a throne as the judge does, and he would take these notes. ... I asked him, what did you write when you saw Gates in this deposition on this day? He said, well, I wrote and he pulled [it out] and he showed me what he wrote.
—Ken Auletta with Margaret Warner, NewsHour, PBS, February 26, 2001

violate antitrust laws. Almost immediately, Microsoft filed an appeal.

On June 7, Judge Jackson dealt Microsoft the worst blow imaginable. He ruled in favor of splitting Microsoft into two companies. The last time the corporate world saw a similar fate handed down to an industry giant was in 1984 to AT&T Corporation. Twenty-four hours later Jackson's quotes landed in print. They would trigger his downfall.

First the *Wall Street Journal* quoted Jackson on Microsoft's legal brief that proposed changes to the government's break-up plan: "Were the Japanese allowed to propose the terms of their surrender? The government won the case."

The next day, the *New York Times* quoted Jackson as saying, "I am not aware of any case authority that says I have to give them any due process at all. The case is over. They lost." On Gates' deposition, the paper quoted Jackson as saying, "Bill Gates' testimony is inherently without credibility and if you can't believe this guy, who else can you believe?"

There were more ill-considered remarks, and they were published in the January 15, 2001, issue of the *New Yorker* magazine. Jackson compared Microsoft executives to "gangland killers" and "drug traffickers." As Ken Auletta explained, "Jackson believed that Gates & Co.'s 'crime' was hubris—a refusal to acknowledge that the nation's antitrust laws applied to them. He was only half joking when he told me, 'If I were able to propose a remedy of my devising, I'd require Mr. Gates to write a book report.' The assignment, Jackson said, would be a recent biography of Napoleon, and he went on, 'Because I think he has a Napoleonic concept of himself and his company, an arrogance that derives from power and unalloyed success, with no leavening hard experience, no reverses.'"

In 1982, AT&T Corporation agreed to divest itself of 22 local Bell telephone operating companies. It had taken the Justice Department eight years of legal wrangling to end the company's dominance over local and long distance phone service.

In 1890, the Sherman Anti-Trust Act was passed by Congress, but it was largely ineffective because of the imprecise language. Other laws, including the Clayton Antitrust Act (1914) and the Robinson-Patman Act (1936), strengthened the role of government in regulating businesses.

Judge Jackson's comments—made when the trial was still in progress—presented a clear violation of three rules from the Code of Conduct for United States Judges. Jackson was now as controversial as his rulings.

On February 28, 2001, the *Washington Post* posed the question, "After 78 days of trial, two days of argument before an appeals court, and enough books to fill a library shelf, there are few mysteries that linger in the government's antitrust prosecution of Microsoft Corp. Except this one: Why did Judge Thomas Penfield Jackson regularly share caustic opinions with reporters?" In its June 28 issue, *Time* magazine seemed to have the answer: "Jackson was not the first (anyone remember Lance Ito?), nor will he be the last. But his was a particularly benign form of narcissism. ... The lure of seeing his opinions printed verbatim in the *New Yorker* and the *Wall Street Journal* would be a heady tonic for anyone who moves in the power circles of Washington, D.C., let alone a district court judge in the autumn of his years."

A month later, four floors above Jackson's courtroom, a panel of judges from the U.S. Court of Appeals heard Microsoft's challenge. When it was time to admonish Jackson's conduct, they didn't hold back, although he was conspicuously absent for the verbal lashing. "We don't run off our mouths in a pejorative way," said Chief Judge Harry Edwards. "Good heavens, is that what judges do? They take preferred reporters in?"

A year later, the Federal Appeals Court struck down the antitrust rulings against Microsoft and removed Judge Jackson from the case, although they found "no evidence of actual bias." In a 7-0 decision to reverse his order to split Microsoft, the court cited Jackson's statements to reporters in their ruling. They included a final dig, calling Judge Jackson's

---

Naiveté: the state or quality of being inexperienced or unsophisticated, especially in being artless, credulous, or uncritical.
—*The American Heritage Dictionary of the English Language*, 4th Edition

Falsus in uno, falsus in omnibus ... untrue in one thing, untrue in everything ... I don't subscribe to that as absolutely true. But it does lead one to suspicion. It's a universal human experience. If someone lies to you once, how much else can you credit is the truth?
—Judge Thomas Penfield Jackson, "For Antitrust Judge, Trust or Lack of It Really Was the Issue," *Wall Street Journal*, June 8, 2000

ethical violations "deliberate, egregious, and flagrant," noting, "public confidence in the judicial process cannot survive when judges pander to the press."

The fact that Jackson had asked reporters for an embargo to delay publication was proof to the panel that he knew his remarks were improper. Judge Learned Hand found Jackson's transgression a sign of a greater weakness. He lamented somewhat poetically about "this America of ours where the passion for publicity is a disease, and where swarms of foolish tawdry moths dash with rapture into its consuming fire."

The Department of Justice pushed for a quick remedy, even though the Court of Appeals agreed that Microsoft had repeatedly engaged in monopolistic practices. Soon a settlement was reached. (Microsoft faced multiple challenges in Europe until agreements were reached in 2009.)

Judge Jackson went on to hear other cases, but they paled in comparison. In 2002, he wrote a commentary in the *Legal Times* seemingly in defense of his own conduct, arguing that judges should respond openly to questions about their decisions. In his words, "Any 'appearance of impartiality' conveyed by a judge's silence may be an illusion. A reputation for candor is a better gauge of integrity than a reputation of silence."

Judge Jackson's "candor" compromised the government's case and hurt his reputation. He learned the hard way that in the dance of media seduction, the interviewer and the subject only seem to be moving as one.

15 Minutes of Fame

Q: Did you really say that everybody is going to be famous for 15 minutes?

WARHOL: Um, well, I think everybody is.

Q: You told me one time that you didn't say that.

WARHOL: Uh, no, I was being funny, then I said every 15 minutes someone will be famous.

—Andy Warhol, "Andy Warhol: A Documentary Film," *American Masters*, PBS, 2006

Mastering Rule 13

Ignorantia juris non excusat. That's Latin for "ignorance of the law excuses no one from prosecution." The same goes for interviews. Ignorance of the interviewing trade won't excuse you from exposure.

Remember, you are never alone when you are alone with a reporter. The intimate chats and talk of book deals had all the hallmarks of a classic seduction. Jackson had been led into his indiscretion by masters of the game. Even for a man of his stature, the temptation to share his thoughts proved too great.

Avoid the fate of the indiscreet subject. In the summer of 2010, four-star General Stanley McChrystal was relieved of his command in Afghanistan after he and his staff reportedly vented their frustrations to a freelance reporter on assignment for *Rolling Stone* magazine. The article, headlined "The Runaway General," was so sensational it put the White House in near-crisis mode for forty-eight hours. The soldiers' quotes were scathing in their put-down of the non-military leaders, including the vice president and the president's national security advisor. The fact that civilian supervision of the military is what allows democracies to endure seemed lost on the career soldiers. McChrystal will have years to reflect on how a thirty-four-year career buckled under the weight of a few words. After his resignation,

When you get out of bed in the morning and think about what you want to do that day, ask yourself whether you'd like others to read about it on the front page of tomorrow's newspaper. You'll probably do things a little differently if you keep that in mind.
—Warren Buffett, chairman of Berkshire Hathaway, "My Golden Rule," CNNMoney, 2005

the general began the journey with an honest admission. "My service did not end as I would have wished," he said.

Do not treat journalists as confidants and friends because they're not. They may like you, but more important for journalists is that you like them. In the introduction to her penetrating work, *The Journalist and the Murderer*, Janet Malcolm writes, "On reading the article or book in question, he [the subject] has to face the fact that the journalist—who seemed so friendly and sympathetic, so keen to understand him fully, so remarkably attuned to his vision of things—never had the slightest intention of collaborating with him on his story but always intended to write a story of his own."

Joan Didion offers another harsh assessment in her best-selling book *Slouching Towards Bethlehem*, writing, "My only advantage as a reporter is that I am so physically small, so temperamentally unobtrusive, and so neurotically inarticulate that people tend to forget that my presence runs counter to their best interest. And it always does. This is one last thing to remember: Writers are always selling someone out."

Observe, while reporters are not sorcerers trying to entrap you, they will never stop you from entrapping yourself. It's hard not to feel you are the center of the universe when the microphone or scribe is recording your every word. No doubt, that's how Jackson felt. However, when Ken Auletta was asked at a book signing if he had any ethical concerns about "allowing" Judge Jackson to speak out as he did, Auletta spoke for all journalists when he said, "I couldn't stop smiling. I mean, is he crazy? I said, you know, my job is to get people to talk to me, not to shut them up."

The theme of betrayal stalks Truman Capote's legacy. Among other things, he led the killers—particularly Smith—to think he cared about them and would assist in their defense and appeals. All he ever really cared about, however, was transfusing their lives onto the page—writing and finishing his book.
—Richard Cohen, on Truman Capote's predatory friendships with Perry Smith and Richard Hickock, the subjects of *In Cold Blood*, "The Lasting Art of Betrayal," *Washington Post*, October 6, 2005

Don't meet with a reporter in secret. Bob Woodward and Carl Bernstein's "Deep Throat" of Watergate fame set the gold standard for risk versus reward. As a source, you will want to cooperate with the media only to the extent that it's in your or the public's interest to do so. Journalists are not indebted to their sources. They don't "owe" you good coverage. Also, don't be overly impressed because the reporter has a well-known byline, or is writing a book or works for a marquee publication.

Beware of the terms journalists use for "off the record." A pre-interview is normally conducted over the telephone and is not for publication. This is the time for the reporters to scope out the developing story. This is the time for you to ask questions. What is the nature of the interview? What kind of information will be required? You will want to know who else will be interviewed, the news hook for the story, the deadline, and so on. No matter if the session is called a pre-interview, a backgrounder (none of the information or quotes will be attributed to you), or an information session to help educate the reporter on a subject (again, no quotes, no attribution), do not say anything you wouldn't want to see published. While the "gentlemen's agreement" of confidentiality between the subject and the reporter may still exist, never, ever give the benefit of the doubt to anyone who works in a newsroom.

Interviews take place in real time. Don't expect the reporter to honor an embargo if what you have said is news. In fact, Judge Jackson's embargo was honored by the publications. The trial was over, but the legal process was not. This was the devastating detail that Jackson failed to appreciate.

If a federal judge wants to talk to a reporter—with full knowledge that the lowly scribe is sitting there with a pen and pad taking down his words—anyone who failed to do the interview would be drummed out of the profession and have to do something really desperate, like become a lawyer. Thomas Penfield Jackson is a big boy. ... But he took a risk, and the appeals court was certainly within its rights by slapping him down.
—Howard Kurtz, washingtonpost.com, July 2, 2001

Microsoft's successful appeal was based on evidence of Jackson's bias in media interviews during the trial. In the era of "breaking news" 24/7, the concept of an embargo is mostly a thing of the past. Assume that you are speaking in real time—and possibly only minutes away from disaster.

Tactic

If you wish to cooperate with reporters who may be requesting more information than it is prudent to give them, ask that the questions be emailed. This way you can consider your responses in advance. If the situation is evolving as it was for Judge Jackson, hold off sending your response until it is safe to do so. Conducting interviews by email is an accepted practice for busy people and for those who want to be cautious.

Game Face Conduct

An interview is not an occasion to settle scores or vent your frustrations with the way things are or should be. Journalists will love you for it, but your pleasure is likely to be short lived. Judge Jackson's remarks about Bill Gates made for colorful copy, but in the end words are a reflection of the speaker's character and judgment. They continue to define that person long after the events themselves have faded into history.

Q: What are some of the most difficult ethical issues you've faced as a journalist? BERNSTEIN: The most important ethical issues and the most difficult ones are the human ones because a reporter has enormous power to hurt people.
—Carl Bernstein, *Big Think*, July 2010

And Finally

Tony Hayward, the former chief executive officer of British Petroleum (BP) admitted to the BBC during a November 8, 2010, interview that BP was "not prepared" to deal with the media scrutiny following the massive oil spill in the Gulf of Mexico. The explosion of the Deepwater Horizon rig on

April 20, 2010 killed eleven workers and sent five million barrels of oil gushing into the ocean before the well was capped months later. Hayward said he had been "demonized" and "vilified" by "the media frenzy." It sounded like criticism of the press. Yet it was Hayward's insensitivity and public whining that defined his communication during the crisis.

His tenure as CEO ended October 1, 2010. Media observers say that Hayward torpedoed his job back in May, during an interview with Fox News. While apologizing to Gulf residents for the disruption, Hayward said, "There's no one who wants this thing over with more than I do, you know, I'd like my life back." His was the sound bite of the day, widely reported on both sides of the Atlantic. Hayward told the BBC, "If I had done a degree at RADA [The Royal Academy of Dramatic Art] rather than a degree in geology, I may have done better, but I'm not certain it would've changed the outcome. But certainly the perception of myself may have been different." It was another telling remark. Hayward was equating the language of leadership with playacting.

Never Speak Ill of the Competition

We are judged by the company we keep and what we say about others, especially during interviews. The media thrive on conflict and controversy, framing the worlds of business, sports, and entertainment as highly personal rivalries with winners and losers. You'll know you've made it if you're being asked to trash the other guy. Television host Dick Cavett touched off a celebrated feud with one of his faux-innocent questions. His guest used the occasion to settle an old score.

Literary Ladies

The only one I can think of is a holdover like Lillian Hellman, who I think is tremendously overrated, a bad writer, and a dishonest writer, but she really belongs to the past. ... I said once in some interview that every word she writes is a lie, including "and" and "the."
—Mary McCarthy

From its inception with Steve Allen in 1954, the late-night talk show has been a staple of American television. In the fall of 1979, *The Dick Cavett Show* was in its second season on the PBS affiliate WNET, opposite NBC's *The Tonight Show* with the legendary host Johnny Carson. Dick Cavett was known for droll one-liners and his conversational interview style. His subjects included artists, intellectuals, and writers not normally seen on television. One such guest was Mary McCarthy. Cavett had been looking forward to conversing with the sixty-seven-year-old writer and critic. "She was lively, witty, opinionated, and striking on camera," he would later remark.

McCarthy authored the 1963 bestselling novel, *The Group*, which told the story of classmates at the prominent liberal arts college Vassar, and how their lives unfolded. The book was racy for the time and Hollywood called with a movie deal. By the late seventies, McCarthy was better known in more rarefied circles for her essays on incendiary topics such as sexual liberation, Vietnam, and Watergate. The day

Libel vs. Slander
Libel is the published or broadcast form of defamation, whereas slander is oral defamation.

she appeared on the Cavett show, the host had received a program note. It read, "Miss McCarthy asked if you'd let her say a few words about a young writer she feels is underrated." During the interview, Cavett instead asked McCarthy to name some *overrated* writers.

CAVETT: *Who are some authors who are overrated, and we could do without, given a limited amount of time?*
MCCARTHY: *I don't think we have those anymore.*
CAVETT: *We don't have the overpraised writer anymore?*
MCCARTHY: *At least I'm not aware of it. The only one I can think of is a holdover like Lillian Hellman, who I think is tremendously overrated, a bad writer, and a dishonest writer, but she really belongs to the past.*
CAVETT: *What is dishonest about [Hellman]?*
MCCARTHY: *Everything. I said once in some interview that every word she writes is a lie, including "and" and "the."*

From the audience came a longish "ooh" and some laughter. The conversation moved on, with guest and host having indulged in some "obvious"—or so they thought— hyperbole.

On the nights of January 24 and 25, the interview hit the airwaves. Playwright Lillian Hellman was at her Manhattan townhouse in bed, frail from emphysema and half blind from glaucoma. With her television tuned to *The Dick Cavett Show* and her hearing still intact, Hellman caught the humiliating put-down. Outraged, she made a phone call to her lawyer, Ephraim London. Three weeks later, McCarthy received some stunning news: Hellman was suing her, WNET, and host Dick Cavett for 2.5 million dollars. The tone was set by London's description of the media moment as "a televised

Even McCarthy's one-liner about Hellman's honesty has a made-for-television ring, in that it [television] traffics in reputation, not issues.
—Carol Brightman, *Writing Dangerously: Mary McCarthy and Her World*, 1992

program in which Miss McCarthy appeared to tout her most recent unsuccessful novel."

Cavett invited Hellman on the show to have her say but she declined. The seventy-two-year-old writer much preferred going after McCarthy wielding the law. Her suit claimed that McCarthy had uttered a statement that was "false, made with ill-will, with malice, with knowledge of its falsity, with careless disregard of its truth, and with the intent to injure the plaintiff personally and professionally."

The story was catnip to the intellectual set, given the professional rivalry between the two women who had little contact except as occupants on literary lists. Lillian Hellman had been born into money and over the years moved among the literati. She emerged as a writer in the time of Ernest Hemingway, William Faulkner, and Dashiell Hammett, the mystery writer with whom she shared a thirty-year relationship. Hellman's plays "The Little Foxes" and "The Children's Hour" had received critical acclaim; each was later adapted into a film with stars Bette Davis and Audrey Hepburn, respectively. In contrast, McCarthy, who was seven years Hellman's junior and something of a femme fatale in her day, was an orphan raised by relatives. The thrice-married McCarthy, never wealthy, earned a respectable living as a writer. While she had published thirteen novels since her first, they were now largely forgotten.

The antipathy between Hellman and McCarthy was also marked by similarities. Each had a major success before thirty and was passionately involved in left-leaning politics. In 1952, Hellman was subpoenaed by the House Un-American Activities Committee over her links with the Communist Party. Hellman set the stage for her testimony by sending a letter, declaring dramatically that she would answer

However, the judge dismissed the action against Mr. Cavett, finding that he was not involved in the preparation or the editing of the program.
—Marcia Chambers, "Lillian Hellman Wins Round in Suit," *New York Times*, May 11, 1984

questions but would not divulge information on others "to cut my conscience to fit this year's fashions." When brought before HUAC, she pleaded the Fifth.

Now, Hellman was organizing for a different kind of fight. McCarthy had kicked her when she was down and Hellman was intent on besting McCarthy. She would sap her finances and show her nemesis that this "holdover" would not be undone.

McCarthy's lawyer, Benjamin O'Sullivan, argued that her remark on the Cavett show was literary criticism of a public figure—an act protected by the First Amendment. Over the years, Hellman had become known for her fierce public support of the First Amendment. And her celebrity status was reinforced when, in 1977, actress Jane Fonda played her in the Oscar-winning film *Julia*, adapted from Hellman's bestselling memoir *Pentimento*. And then there was the advertising campaign for Blackglama furs that featured Hellman as one of its famous models. She had posed wearing a mink coat, cigarette in hand, her rugged face showing its years under the tagline: "What becomes a legend most?" Still, Hellman's lawyer rejected the "public figure" argument, countering, "The First Amendment guarantees the right of speech. It doesn't guarantee the right to lie about someone."

As brawls go, this one was high brow. In the *New York Times*, Michiko Kakutani reported that Hellman once referred to McCarthy's fictions as those of "a lady magazine writer," and McCarthy described Hellman's plays as works of "oily virtuosity." With battle lines drawn, writers and editors took sides. "I might have at least granted Lillian Hellman the 'thes' and 'ands,'" said Irving Howe, co-editor of the quarterly *Dissent*. "But aside from that, I'm sure Mary's right." (Others in the pro-McCarthy camp included Susan Sontag,

Asked if she thought Miss Hellman's work dishonest, Mrs. [Lionel] Trilling replied demurely, "Let's say she's a gifted writer of fictions."
—Michiko Kakutani, "Hellman-McCarthy Libel Suit Stirs Old Antagonisms," *New York Times*, March 19, 1980

Norman Podhoretz, and Diana Trilling.) Richard Poirier, a former editor of *Partisan Review* and a friend of Hellman's, said McCarthy's attack was, "dizzy without being funny at all, and since she claims to have said it before, what's interesting is that it should now be getting such publicity."

The clash prompted author Norman Mailer to write an open letter appealing to both women to put aside their differences. His peacemaking effort fell flat. However, Hellman at one point agreed to drop the suit if McCarthy would apologize publicly. McCarthy refused saying, "That would be lying."

McCarthy's comment dismissing Hellman was made in a matter of seconds, but the stand-off went unresolved for four years. On May 10, 1984, McCarthy got bad news: New York Supreme Court Judge Harold Baer, Jr., denied her motion to dismiss the case. He rejected McCarthy's defense that her remark was literary criticism of a public figure. "To call someone dishonest, to say to a national television audience that every word she writes is a lie, seems to fall on the actionable side of the line—outside what has come to be known as the 'marketplace of ideas,'" ruled Baer. McCarthy appealed.

Though she always said she regarded Hellman's plays as "tedious and contrived and not worth the bother," McCarthy was now forced to read every word written by her adversary to defend herself.

Hellman won the preliminary round, but by launching the suit she unwittingly subjected her entire body of work to scrutiny. If literary insiders ever whispered about her dishonesty as a writer, they were now publicly debating her veracity and how she had cunningly fudged it in two of her memoirs: *An Unfinished Woman* and *Pentimento*. Public opinion was leaning toward her guilt, with dramatic

I don't want to sound uncharitable about my critics. Indeed, I appreciate their attention. After all, a man's detractors work for him tirelessly and for free.
—Marshall McLuhan,
Playboy, March 1969

evidence that Hellman had appropriated the story of an expatriate American heiress, Muriel Gardiner-Buttinger. A section in *Pentimento*, entitled "Julia," was found to be remarkably similar to the true-life story of Gardiner-Buttinger, who heroically fought fascism in 1930s Vienna.

Her world in turmoil, Hellman died of cardiac arrest at age seventy-seven at her Martha's Vineyard home on June 30, 1984. Hellman's lawsuit against McCarthy was dropped by the executors of her estate. But as Hellman had planned, the litigious brawling took its toll on McCarthy's finances and on her health. That same year, McCarthy was awarded the Edward MacDowell Medal for her writings. She still dared to flaunt her feistiness during a telephone interview with Samuel G. Freedman of the *New York Times*. Of Hellman, she said: "I didn't want her to die. I wanted her to lose in court. I wanted her around for that."

Five years later, at age seventy-nine, McCarthy's contrarian voice was silenced by lung cancer. As it was with Lillian Hellman when she died, Mary McCarthy's obituary made reference to the other woman and the war of words that had cast such a deep shadow on their final years.

Everybody's memory is tricky and mine's a little trickier than most, I guess.

—Lillian Hellman, "A Still Unfinished Woman: A Conversation with Lillian Hellman," *Rolling Stone*, February 1977

Mastering Rule 14

Speaking of the
Competition

Remember, reporters are on a perpetual quest for opposition. This is why they phrase questions the way they do, comparing and contrasting opposite points of view into "rival" camps. Be prepared to present yourself or your interest in contrast to someone or something else, but resist the invitation to criticize.

Naughty

I can't read him because he's such a bad writer. ...
I don't think it's a war because you can't have a war between a pawn and a king, can you? ... He's a journalist; ... he can't create a character.
—John Irving, on Tom Wolfe, *Hot Type*, CBC, December 17, 1999

There's such an exaggeration of protest that underneath the person means the opposite. ... *A Man in Full* frightened him [Irving], the same way it frightened John Updike and Norman Mailer. Frightened them. Panicked them. They're my Three Stooges: Larry, Curly, and Moe—Updike, Mailer, and Irving.
—Tom Wolfe, on John Irving, *Hot Type*, CBC, January 28, 2000

Always begin and end with your own position. Do this when asked whether you agree with the stance of a "rival," real or imagined by the media. It is likely you may be hearing the other camp's position for the first time during the interview. As well, do not become a surrogate for the opposition. Repeat as often as necessary, "I can't speak for Ms. Hellman," or better still, "You'll have to ask Ms. Hellman that question."

Avoid blanket characterizations of others. Calling someone a liar is a serious matter. Indeed, any comment that defames someone's character is off limits. If it becomes necessary to address or challenge an adversarial word or deed, be brief, factual, and specific. Your response should not be greater than what you are countering. The goal is to blunt the criticism rather than expand the conflict.

Don't rush to debate a "rival" for an orchestrated encounter. This may be necessary for politicians, but it is doubtful that your interest will be served by a staged confrontation. In this case, it was shrewd of Cavett to invite Hellman to tell her side of the story (and possibly avoid a lawsuit) and equally shrewd of Hellman to decline. For Hellman, the damage had been done. It's an accepted wisdom that corrections issued by news organizations never have the same reach or audience members who read or heard the erroneous information in the first place.

Know when it's time to withdraw without further comment. Feuds are made in media heaven because they keep controversies going. This happens when the subjects keep talking even when it's no longer in their interest to do so.

Keep your vocabulary in neutral when asked about "rivals." In May 2009, the media began reporting on a "fierce battle" between the BlackBerry-maker cofounder Jim Balsillie and National Hockey League Commissioner Gary Bettman. The story began when Balsillie announced his intention to buy the financially struggling Phoenix Coyotes directly from the majority shareholder. He planned to move the team from Glendale, Arizona, to Hamilton, Ontario, in Canada. The NHL commissioner opposed the move given "the tactic" and "the challenge to league rules." The *National Post* called the relationship between the two men "contentious." The back story included the fact that Balsillie had failed on two previous occasions to buy NHL teams for Hamilton. There was also the financial impact the sale would have on the Toronto Maple Leafs franchise, located only forty miles from Hamilton. In the end, the sale was blocked by an Arizona bankruptcy judge.

The situation had all the makings of an epic smackdown, but the two men stick-handled their interviews like pros. Balsillie glided by questions about Bettman, calling him "the

Naughty

His movies are perfect backgrounds for fashion models. Maybe there aren't backgrounds that good in *Vogue*, but there ought to be.
—Orson Welles, on the films of Michelangelo Antonioni, *Playboy*, March 1967

The eminent explorer David Livingstone had three boyish habits, two of them naughty, it was disclosed yesterday. He slagged off his rivals, carved his initials on trees, and sealed messages in bottles. Also in the collection is Livingstone's attack on fellow explorer Sir Richard Burton. "Burton is the most awful ruffian," he wrote to a colleague. "I don't believe that Burton was ever at Mecca."
—John Ezard, "Dr. Livingstone, I presume ... the naughty one," *Guardian*, February 18, 2004

Commissioner" to avoid even saying his name. For his part, Bettman took shots at the multi-millionaire's attempt to circumvent the league while sidestepping questions about Balsillie himself. For Bettman and Balsillie, it was nothing personal, or so they claimed—and demonstrated with words.

Tactic

Show your game face when the attention is on another speaker. Do not fall into the habit of nodding your head—or smiling or laughing along—when another person is speaking. It could look as if you are agreeing to a response you haven't fully heard. Also, don't shake your head in disagreement when others are speaking or making statements during interviews, panel discussions, or debates. It's not only distracting; it could appear adversarial and invite the same discourteous behavior when you are speaking.

Game Face Conduct

Be gracious in victory as well as defeat. There are many benign things McCarthy could have said upon hearing the news of Hellman's death, but she chose to keep the rivalry going. According to her biographer Frances Kiernan, even McCarthy's husband, James R. West, thought she had gone too far. "I regret her public statement," said West. "I thought it was a bit gross myself."

And Finally

McCarthy admitted that she had said the same thing about Hellman before. If she had, it must have been during a newspaper interview. Is the medium itself a factor in the creation of defining moments? In his pioneering book, *No Sense of Place: The Impact of Electronic Media on Social*

Behavior, Joshua Meyrowitz makes the case for the differences between print and television. He states, "Because of the rich expressive dimensions of television, interviews on television are completely different from print interviews. On television, even a 'no comment' or a long pause is a meaningful and significant 'answer.' ... It shows the speaker's response to the situation ... even though the response is essentially nonverbal." For Meyrowitz, this helps to explain the contradiction whereby a voter will give a politician a low mark on job performance but a high score on personal appeal. Such behavior, according to Meyrowitz, would be "unthinkable if the voters only had access to transcripts of the candidates' speeches and policy statements; it only makes sense when the voters feel they 'know' the candidates personally."

Meyrowitz's theories were given life during the 2016 Republican Party presidential primaries. Seventeen candidates entered the race behind headliners Ted Cruz, Jeb Bush and Marco Rubio. During their debates, Donald Trump, the billionaire businessman and television host, overwhelmed his political rivals with personal attacks and anti-beltway rhetoric.

Trump's "platform" was a string of populist messages delivered with a reckless nonchalance that passed for authenticity. He dominated the news cycle with conduct that both disgusted and inspired voters. This included the use of his Twitter account to fudge facts and insult anyone who crossed him. It was personality politics taken to a whole new level.

Nice

Ernest Hemingway, I think, is the greatest living writer of English. He took that place when Kipling died. Next comes Thomas Wolfe and then Faulkner and Dos Passos.
—F. Scott Fitzgerald, "The Other Side of Paradise, Scott Fitzgerald, 40, Engulfed in Despair," *New York Post*, September 25, 1936

He [Malcolm X] is very articulate, as you say, but I totally disagree with many of his political and philosophical views—at least insofar as I understand where he now stands. I don't want to seem to sound self-righteous, or absolutist, or that I think I have the only truth, the only way. Maybe he *does* have some of the answers.
—Martin Luther King, Jr., *Playboy*, January 1965

The media greatly enabled Trump, embracing the spectacle to give him vast swaths of real estate on air, online and in print.
—David Folkenflik, N P R media correspondent, npr.org, May 5, 2016

Don't Confuse Talking with Communicating

The more you talk, the less you communicate. Consider the fate of William Ginsburg during his four-month odyssey in the U.S. capitol. At the height of the Clinton-Lewinsky affair, Ginsburg was generating more ink than the president. With his many mixed messages and sensational sound bites, he was in high demand. But as Ginsburg lost sight of his communication objectives, he lost his client and soon the journalists stopped calling.

Lost in the Green Room

The press overwhelmed me. I'm not going to tell you I was good at it or I was bad at it, but I will tell you it was overwhelming. ... It became apparent to me that I needed media help.
—William Ginsburg

On January 16, 1998, former White House intern Monica Lewinsky set out for the Pentagon City Mall in Washington, D.C. She had been invited to lunch by a friend and former colleague, Linda Tripp. Within minutes of her arrival, Lewinsky was approached by FBI agents and escorted to room 1012 of the Ritz-Carlton Hotel. With Tripp in tow, she was grilled by six deputy prosecutors and offered immunity for details of her affair with the president of the United States, William "Bill" Clinton. Only then did Lewinsky realize that in a stunning betrayal, her confidant had set the trap after taping their conversations.

Just hours before, independent counsel Ken Starr had gained approval to include Lewinsky in an expanded probe into the sexual harassment suit against then Governor Clinton, filed by Paula Jones. Lewinsky had already signed an affidavit denying she and the president ever had a sexual relationship. After the twelve-hour ordeal, Lewinsky called her parents. Her father contacted William H. Ginsburg, a family friend and medical malpractice lawyer based in her hometown of Beverly Hills. The next day, Ginsburg was on a plane to Washington, D.C.

The "green room" is an area where talk show guests can relax or refresh their make-up while waiting to be called on to the set. The tradition started in the theatre, where historically these rooms were painted green.

On the following day the conservative Internet site the Drudge Report broke the "world exclusive" that a twenty-three-year-old White House intern had carried on a sexual affair with the president. The report tore a path through cyberspace. Three days later, Lewinsky was named in the *Washington Post*—the same newspaper that in 1972 broke the Watergate story that forced President Richard Nixon's resignation. The *Post* reported Starr was pursuing allegations that the president suborned perjury, made false statements, and obstructed justice by encouraging Lewinsky to lie under oath in the Paula Jones case.

Hours after the story broke, Clinton was interviewed on PBS. Host Jim Lehrer jumped on the breaking story and asked the president, "Did you have an improper relationship with Lewinsky? Did you have sexual relations with this young woman?" Clinton denied the allegations, insisting, "There is no improper relationship."

Inquiring minds were learning that the Washington chapter of Monica's Lewinsky's life began with a summer internship in 1995. Thereafter Lewinsky was hired by the White House and worked in the Office of Legislative Affairs, handling correspondence. She delivered items to the Oval Office where, on occasion, she would run into Clinton. By April 1996, Lewinsky was reassigned to the Pentagon, bringing an end to her secret year-and-a-half affair with the president. Feeling rejected over the transfer, Lewinsky began sharing her frustrations with co-worker Linda Tripp, a former White House staffer in the George H. W. Bush administration. Tripp, soon to become the world's best-known tattletale, provided prosecutors with twenty hours of secret recordings.

The media chased the salacious details of the biggest story to hit Washington since Watergate. At a January 26 press conference on the eve of his State of the Union address, a forceful Clinton told reporters, "I want to say one thing to the American people. I want you to listen to me. I'm going to say this again. I did not have sexual relations with that woman, Miss Lewinsky."

Lewinsky was center stage, but her lawyer was the one doing the talking. William Ginsburg was negotiating to secure his client's immunity from prosecution in return for her testimony. After the discussions stalled, Ginsburg stepped up his media campaign.

His ability to communicate a compelling narrative on behalf of Lewinsky was now key, but the lack of a strategy became apparent as his curious statements began to make news. On January 27, in an interview with *Yediot Ahronot*, Israel's largest daily, Ginsburg was quoted as saying, "Clinton is very positive toward Israel and the Jews, and Monica and I are Jews. ... I don't want the president to resign. Who knows who will come after Clinton and how he will deal with Israel?"

Ginsburg's messages went from oddities to indiscretions. In an apparent reference to Lewinsky, he told the *Washington Post*, "There are people who talk a lot and as part of the scenario, peccadilloes, they may tell fibs, lies, exaggerations, oversell." To *Time* magazine—about Lewinsky—he said, "I kissed that girl's inner thighs when she was six days old. I said, 'Look at those little *pulkes*.'"

Susan Estrich, law professor and writer, noted Ginsburg's "embarrassingly bad job" in the *Los Angeles Times*. Meanwhile, the *Pittsburgh Post-Gazette* couldn't refrain from asking flat out, "Is there a method to his madness or is it just madness?" The more Ginsburg talked, the more observers wondered if he was up to the job. Legal experts debated if he

A computer search found 29 appearances on major talk shows, which does not count the innumerable interviews he gave for daily news programs.
—Peter Baker, "Ginsburg's Role Shrinks as Starr Nears Decision," *Washington Post*, May 24, 1998

intentionally skewed impressions about Lewinsky's truthfulness to weaken the impact of her recorded conversations with Tripp. Still these same observers were baffled by Ginsburg's off-the-wall comments, given his background.

Ginsburg had amassed thirty years of litigation experience, mostly defending corporate and institutional clients and winning the majority of his cases. "He has the ability to understand the heart of an issue very quickly, and an ability to communicate with juries on a true common-sense level," said Ginsburg's partner, George Stephan.

Only one month into his job, Ginsburg the outsider had taken the media power game to new heights. The *Washington Post* described how he, having completed a television interview, "pulled out his beeper and began reading off the latest messages from journalists beseeching him for interviews. 'Call Mike Wallace,' Ginsburg recited aloud, referring to the *60 Minutes'* correspondent. 'My new best friend,' he observed." He was paged during a meal with Wallace by ABC's Diane Sawyer, and he spent Super Bowl Sunday in the home of CNN's Wolf Blitzer, reported *Newsweek*.

The self-described "most famous person in the world" accomplished something unprecedented. Ginsburg appeared on all five networks on a single Sunday. Harvard law professor Alan Dershowitz told CNN's *Late Edition*, "I hate to say this because Bill Ginsburg seems like such a nice man, but he's way, way over his head. ... He's negotiating in public. He has made a number of statements detrimental to his client ... and I think she's in real jeopardy as a result of that."

Indeed, Lewinsky's legal standing was precarious. By March of 1998, a grand jury was listening to Tripp's secret recordings. At the same time, Ginsburg and lawyer Nathaniel Speights continued to battle Starr on whether a binding

In Principle:

Public Relations is the practice of cultivating relationships with the media in order to generate favorable coverage. It is known as "earned media" in contrast to paid advertising.

Interviews with William Ginsburg, which aired on Sunday, February 1, 1998 on all five U.S. networks, set a record. The rare feat is known in media circles as the "Full-Ginsburg."

1. *Meet the Press*, NBC
2. *Face the Nation*, CBS
3. *This Week*, ABC
4. *Fox News Sunday*, Fox
5. *Late Edition*, CNN

immunity deal actually existed. Ginsburg, meanwhile, took to pulling Lewinsky out of her Watergate apartment and parading her around town. The *New York Times'* William Safire wrote an essay on his encounter with Lewinsky and Ginsburg at the Cosmos Club; the *Washington Post* reported on a sighting of Lewinsky at a basketball game. "Eventually, we had to get her out. ... I felt that this would be an excellent test to show that we weren't afraid," said Ginsburg.

But troubles abounded. Even though a U.S. district judge dismissed the Paula Jones sexual harassment suit against Clinton on April 1, the Starr investigative team gave no indication that it was letting up on its criminal investigation. Then a federal judge ruled that Lewinsky did not have an immunity deal with Ken Starr, despite Ginsburg's proclamations.

Weeks after the no-immunity ruling, on May 24, 1998, the *Washington Post* reported the Lewinsky family had hired Judy Smith, a public relations consultant. Media pundits speculated on the shrinking public role for Ginsburg, pondering aloud if he was on his way out as legal counsel. In response to being cut off from his media supply, the loquacious litigator made a telling admission.

"The press overwhelmed me," he told the *Post.* "I'm not going to tell you I was good at it or I was bad at it. But I will tell you it was overwhelming. ... It became apparent to me that I needed media help." His confession was a little late, particularly since the interview was arranged through the newly hired Smith.

Despite the clamp-down, Ginsburg had yet to have his last indulgence. Frustrated and angry, he wrote a taunting "open letter" to Starr published on May 27 on washingtonpost.com. "Congratulations, Mr. Starr! As a result of your

But the all-Ginsburg, all-the-time show has been canceled. Following widespread criticism that his ubiquitous—and sometimes contradictory—public pronouncements were hurting rather than helping his client, the Lewinsky camp has pulled the plug.
—Peter Baker, "Ginsburg's Role Shrinks as Starr Nears Decision," *Washington Post,* May 24, 1998

callous disregard for cherished constitutional rights, you *may* have succeeded in unmasking a sexual relationship between two consenting adults." The bombshell did even more to splinter Ginsburg's image, as legal experts panned his missive as a colossal blunder.

Days later, on June 2, Ginsburg was replaced as Lewinsky's lawyer in favor of Washington-based insiders Jacob Stein and Plato Cacheris. *Time* magazine reported on their introduction to the media—with a confident-looking Lewinsky standing behind them. The split between Ginsburg and Lewinsky was said to be "by mutual agreement."

Still, the ghost of Ginsburg lingered. During the legal shake-up, editors at *Vanity Fair* were busy poring over copy for their prized coup—a deal brokered by Ginsburg himself. When the magazine ran its six-page photo spread in the July 1998 issue, the world saw Monica Lewinsky in a series of shots from coquettish to sultry. Ginsburg explained to the *Washington Post*, "You have to realize that a twenty-four-year-old girl who is imprisoned, her ego, her libido, her mind imprisoned by Ken Starr and the press ... begins to feel that her self-worth is diminishing. ... So the avuncular friend, the surrogate father, has to figure out ways to get her back to par. One of the ways is to express her beauty." The photo spread infuriated Lewinsky's new team.

That summer, at long last, things improved for Lewinsky. On July 27, she met with Starr's prosecutors in New York and confessed to having had a sexual affair with President Clinton. The former intern refused, however, to say that Clinton directed her to lie about it. The next day lawyers for both sides settled on a full immunity agreement for Lewinsky and her parents. On August 17, the president appeared on national television and admitted the affair.

He saw himself as her surrogate father, yet he never understood her depth of feelings for the president, or the way in which his own inappropriate, and often sexual, comments added to her private pain and public humiliation.
—Andrew Morton, *Monica's Story*, 1999

It would take almost two years for William Ginsburg to make his next television appearance. On CNN's *Larry King Live*, June 14, 2000, Ginsburg conceded his missteps in managing Lewinsky's communications. "Some of the disappointments that I had [was] in realizing how powerful the media is today and how things can become so convoluted," said Ginsburg.

Asked about his infamous showboating, Ginsburg replied, "Well, let's see, I've heard that described as media hound, I've heard it described as megalomaniac. I've heard it described on your show last night as acting like a horse's ass. But no matter how you say it, in the next breath if the question is asked, everyone has to say the following: all of the attention was diverted from Monica. She was never indicted, she was never questioned by Starr or his people while I was on the job, she was never brought before the grand jury and nothing ever happened to her while I was protecting her."

Whatever legal victories Ginsburg was claiming, his scattergun approach to going on the record was a public relations disaster. While he filled newspaper columns and air time with chatter, he failed to deliver a consistent storyline, to advance his client's interest.

Melodrama suited Ginsburg. Because of his ubiquity on the airwaves, Ginsburg made the transformation from conscientious advocate to national joke faster than almost anyone in history.
—Jeffrey Toobin, *A Vast Conspiracy: The Real Story of a Sex Scandal That Nearly Brought Down a President*, 2000

Mastering Rule 15

Remember, journalism is a business with an overriding bias that favors profitability over personalities.

Frame messages in a way that advances your position. On Ginsburg's strategy, one must quote German theologian Dietrich Bonhoeffer: "If you get on the wrong train, running down the aisle in the opposite direction really doesn't help." A less frivolous explanation of what went wrong is offered by linguist Deborah Tannen in her book *Framing in Discourse*. According to Tannen, "frames" guide audiences to the appropriate interpretations of events being communicated.

Don't assume because you're talking that you're communicating. Communication isn't what you say; it's what other people hear. William Ginsburg talked a lot, but he lacked a strategic framework and consistent messaging. Nothing he said seemed to build on what he had said before. Ginsburg watchers never knew what to expect from him—or what he expected from his audience.

Silence is not only golden; it is seldom misquoted.
—Robert "Bob" Monkhouse

"Communication, in other words, always makes demands. It always demands that the recipient become somebody, do something, believe something. It always appeals to motivation. Whereas information, like data, makes no demands." And that, according to management guru Peter F. Drucker, is the difference between communication and information. Think of "information" as generic content and "communication" as branded content.

Theme: an implicit or
recurrent idea; a motif.
—*The American Heritage
Dictionary of the English
Language,* 4th Edition

Take it away. This pudding
has no theme.
—Sir Winston Churchill,
during a luncheon, *The
Definitive Wit of Winston
Churchill,* 2009

Use literary themes to make your story memorable. If ever you're in serious trouble, be sure to find a litigator who shares a twin passion for the law and Jane Austen. You will want an advocate who knows the difference between a metaphor and a simile because more than facts, juries love a good story. Ginsburg failed to present a recurring theme or motif in his presentation of Lewinsky. Was Monica Lewinsky a woman betrayed by a malevolent partisan posing as a friend? Or was she collateral damage in a political gun battle between a president and his enemies? We never knew.

Observe the winning ways of defense attorneys. They are adept at presenting different scenarios of the crime than the ones being offered by the prosecution. As trial consultant Amy Singer explained in an issue of the *Trial Diplomacy Journal,* "The trial theme provides essential meaning to the jurors to help them organize and remember case facts. A strong theme will prompt the jurors to look for evidence that supports the theme while ignoring evidence that doesn't. The right theme helps jurors rationalize away all the case conflicts and justify the desired case viewpoint." This point was underscored by Michael Jackson's attorney, Tom Mesereau, during an MSNBC interview on June 22, 2005. In discussing his most famous case he said, "We had a story to tell. We were not going to rely on problems with their witnesses. We had a story to tell. We put on a lot of witnesses ourselves, and we vindicated and cleared Michael Jackson completely."

Make your most important points early and keep it simple. The media do not report complex stories well. Overly convoluted statements and arguments are likely to be misunderstood or lost in translation. It is not a matter of "dummying down." On the contrary, it's an intellectual challenge to turn complicated ideas or arguments into communication that the average person can understand.

Another reason to keep it simple is time, especially in the age of electronic media. The ten-second sound bite is a creation of television news. In June 1973, *Playboy* magazine asked the legendary anchor Walter Cronkite if it was true that someone at CBS News once pasted the transcript of his thirty-minute broadcast into a dummy front page of the *New York Times*, and that the entire show filled less than eight columns. Cronkite responded, "Yes ... we are a front page service. We don't have the time to deal with the back pages at all." And that was decades ago.

Tactic

Know your position and keep to it. There will always be different sides to a story. When giving an interview, set your compass and stay the course. If you present different sides, you will confuse your audience. In addition, circuitous remarks could be edited in ways that distort or bypass your actual position. Leave the responsibility of overall balance to the reporter.

Game Face Conduct

If you're the spokesperson, remember this: Interviews are not about you. They are about the interest of the company, organization, or individual you represent. Everything you say that is not part of a communication plan or message platform could be a distraction or even harmful to the cause. Be charming, be engaging, but never forget why you're there.

The press patiently put up with Mr. Ginsburg's ballooning ego, hoping he'd deliver an exclusive with the Purported Presidential Lollipop. And the California lawyer egged on his panting pursuers, dangling the first print interview to one, the first prime-time interview to another, the first newsmagazine interview to a third.
—Maureen Dowd, "Liberties; Getting the 'Get' of the Century," *New York Times*, June 14, 1998

And Finally

Knowledge is like pie; don't serve too much at once. If you overload your answers, people lose track, then they lose interest. In the 2000 presidential debates with George W. Bush, Vice President Al Gore didn't appear to be listening when the editor in his head was shouting, stop, stop, stop, the audience can't keep up! Gore, a former journalist, congressman, and senator who served two terms as U.S. vice president, seemed to turn his advantage of superior credentials and experience into a disadvantage. How so? Because of his tendency to give people more information than they needed or could take in.

Also, when you overload your answers, you risk appearing as if you are showing off or talking down to your audience. (Gore's audible sighs when Bush was responding were also detrimental.) Many viewers found themselves relating to the less-knowledgeable debater, who became their next president.

Avoid the "Diminished Capacity" Apologia

Nothing becomes a person more than the manner in
which he says, "I'm sorry." Many claim not to know
who, if anyone, they have offended. Others simply evade
blame. In his high-profile apology, actor Mel Gibson was
taking responsibility publicly while avoiding responsibility
personally. With the diminished capacity apologia, a long
list of offenders, including radio host Rush Limbaugh and
comic Michael Richards, apparently were too intoxicated,
too medicated, or too angry to know what they were saying.

The Twinkie Defense

Let me be real clear here, in sobriety, sitting here, in front of you, on national television that I don't believe the Jews are responsible for all the wars in the world. I mean that's an outrageous, drunken statement.
—Mel Gibson

In the early hours of July 28, 2006, actor and film director Mel Gibson was driving along the Pacific Coast Highway in Malibu when he was stopped by Deputy James Mee of the Los Angeles County Sheriff's Department. Gibson's Lexus had been clocked at 87 mph in a 45 mph zone. Mee arrested the actor on suspicion of driving under the influence. Almost immediately, Gibson began expressing concerns about the impending bad publicity. The officer opted to forego the handcuffs. But then Gibson made a dash for his car. Mee chased, apprehended, and then cuffed him. On the ride to the station, Gibson became agitated and increasingly belligerent toward the officer. Gibson's blood-alcohol level was 0.12 percent—exceeding California's 0.08 percent legal limit. He was booked and released on $5,000 bail.

Mea culpa—from Latin—translates to "my fault" or "I am culpable." The words first appeared as an expression of sinfulness used in prayers from the fourteenth century. Nowadays, it's often said in jest to say "I'm sorry."

In the evening, news of Gibson's arrest broke as an exclusive by TMZ, the entertainment website. Despite initial claims from the sheriff's department that the actor was arrested without incident, embarrassing details of the DUI arrest were soon made public. TMZ had an inside source and four pages from Mee's police report.

"TMZ has learned that Mel Gibson went on a rampage when he was arrested Friday on suspicion of drunk driving, hurling religious epithets," the website reported. "Once inside the car, a source directly connected with the case says Gibson began banging himself against the seat."

TMZ went on to describe how Gibson swore profusely at Deputy Mee. "Gibson almost continually [sic] threatened me saying he 'owns Malibu' and will spend all of his money to 'get even' with me. Then Gibson launched into a barrage of anti-Semitic statements: '[expletive] Jews. ... The Jews are responsible for all the wars in the world.' Gibson then asked the deputy, 'Are you a Jew?'" reported TMZ.

Gibson had won over American hearts with his cinematic successes. Now the first man to make *People* magazine's Sexiest Man Alive cover had turned his DUI arrest into an A-list public-relations disaster.

On July 29, the day after his arrest, Gibson released a statement. "The arresting officer was just doing his job and I feel fortunate that I was apprehended before I caused injury to any other person," he said. "I acted like a person completely out of control when I was arrested, and said things that I do not believe to be true and which are despicable. I am deeply ashamed of everything I said, and I apologize to anyone who I have offended."

Not everyone was ready to accept his apology. Two years earlier, Gibson stood at the center of a public storm over his film *The Passion of the Christ*, which he co-wrote, financed, and directed. In the months leading up to its release, some Jewish organizations accused the filmmaker of stoking the flames of anti-Semitism. Calls to boycott the picture, however, fell flat. *The Passion of the Christ* broke records, grossing over $600 million worldwide.

"Never underestimate the power of 'I'm sorry' and the ability of people to forget," said Sean Cassidy, president of Dan Klores Communications. There is a caveat, he said. The tactic will only get a story off the front pages for a while. To wrest the full potential from the public relations cure, it does help, he said, to be sincere.
—Alan Feuer, "When They Say Alcohol Made Me Do It," *New York Times*, October 8, 2006

In light of Gibson's verbal meltdown, charges of anti-Semitism resurfaced.

The Anti-Defamation League issued a statement quoting its national director, Abraham Foxman, saying, "Mel Gibson's apology is unremorseful and insufficient. It's not a proper apology because it does not go to the essence of his bigotry and his anti-Semitism."

Five days after his arrest, both the *Los Angeles Times* and the *New York Times* confirmed the authenticity of the leaked pages from the police report. That same day, Gibson made a second apology. This time his statement addressed the words he spewed at officer Mee: "I want to apologize specifically to everyone in the Jewish community for the vitriolic and harmful words that I said to a law enforcement officer the night I was arrested on a DUI charge." Gibson also appealed to Jewish community leaders to meet with him.

The media gave Gibson's apology a failing grade. Ray Richmond of *Hollywood Reporter* told CNN's *Reliable Sources*, "I don't see sincerity behind that. If there was huge sincerity, he might have said it to the camera himself and wouldn't have ... asked his publicist to throw it out there."

"Mel gives excellent apology when his back is shoved up against the wall and he gets a do-over," wrote Arianna Huffington in the *Huffington Post*. "If these are truly Mel Gibson's feelings, then let me be among the first to welcome him back to the land of the sane. If they are the work of a publicist, I want his name and number. He's the Shakespeare of spin, the Picasso of PR, the Camus of Contrition."

In August, Gibson pleaded no contest to one misdemeanor charge of drunk driving. The judge sentenced him to three years' probation. Gibson was fined and his driver's license was suspended for ninety days.

As a result of TMZ's actions, California Assemblywoman Julia Brownley introduced legislation known as "Mel's Law." Bill AB920 makes it a misdemeanor for peace officers or law enforcement employees to sell privileged information relating to the arrests of high-profile suspects.

If Gibson thought he could now put the transgression behind him, he was mistaken. Many were still pondering those hateful words. Gibson agreed to a two-part interview with Diane Sawyer for ABC's *Good Morning America* to talk about his films and to clear the air. Well, that was the plan.

On October 12, the two met in Gibson's Malibu office. Sawyer asked about the events of that day.

GIBSON: *Well of course, I guess I must have been a little overwrought. That's what happens. Too much pressure, too much work. You do things that go against good judgment. So that's it. A few drinks later and I was in the back of a police car wailing.*

SAWYER: *A few drinks later, do you know how many?*

GIBSON: *No I don't. But I know it was tequila.*

SAWYER: *So how drunk were you?*

GIBSON: *It's not a question of how drunk you are. You're impaired. Your judgment is impaired enough to do insane things like try and drive at high speeds. Even a couple of drinks, you lose all humility.*

Sawyer recounted what Gibson had said, including the remark "Jews are responsible for all the wars in the world."

SAWYER: *Are those words anti-Semitic?*

GIBSON: *Oh, yes. Absolutely. It sounds horrible. And I'm ashamed that came out of my mouth. I'm not that. That's not who I am.*

The next day, Sawyer revisited the incident, this time digging deeper. Gibson began with the Israeli-Hezbollah War,

The "Twinkie defense" was first used by a reporter covering the murder trial of Dan White, the accused killer of San Francisco Mayor George Moscone and Supervisor Harvey Milk. The defense's case during the 1979 trial was diminished capacity—White had suffered from bouts of depression, amounting to "a major mental illness" evidenced by his over-consumption of junk food. The media chose to attribute the depression to Twinkies, the iconic cream-filled confection, and so the "Twinkie defense" was born. It has become a derisive label for any far-fetched criminal defense or apology.

which at the time of his arrest, was in its seventeenth day. For the actor, the conflict had become personal.

GIBSON: *Maybe it was just that very day that Lebanon and Israel were at it. Since I was a kid in the '60s, '70s, '80s, '90s, and now in the new millennium, you can read of an ever-escalating kind of conflagration over there in the Middle East that I remember thinking when I was 20, man, that place is going to drag us all into the black hole, you know, just the difficulty over there."*
SAWYER: *But there's a difference between saying that place is a tinderbox and the constellation of things happening there could take us all down, and saying the Jews are responsible for all the wars.*

Struggling, Gibson delivered what sounded like his bottom line.

GIBSON: *No, no, did I say that? Let me be real clear, here, in sobriety, sitting here, in front of you, on national television, that I don't believe the Jews are responsible for all the wars in the world. I mean that's an outrageous, drunken statement.*

The actor was harboring something else. As Gibson explained, when *The Passion of the Christ* was released in 2004, he was "subjected to a pretty brutal sort of public beating. ... During the course of that, I think I probably had my rights violated in many different ways as an American. You know. As an artist. As a Christian. Just as a human being, you know. I thought I dealt with that stuff. All forgiveness, but, the human heart's a funny thing. Sometimes you can bear the scars of resentment. And it'll come out, you know, when you're overwrought, you take a few drinks."

The film came out. It was released, and you could have heard a pin drop, you know. Even the crickets weren't chirping. But, the other thing I never heard was one single word of apology.
—Mel Gibson, speaking about *The Passion of the Christ* and its detractors, *Good Morning America*, October 13, 2006

If, with this explanation, Gibson was trying to rationalize his actions in July, not everyone found the attempt successful. In fact, the more he explained, the more his critics had to say.

Washington Post columnist Eugene Robinson was skeptical, writing, "Well, I'm sorry about his relapse, too, but I just don't buy the idea that a little tequila, or even a lot of tequila, can somehow turn an unbiased person into a raging anti-Semite—or a racist, or a homophobe, or a bigot of any kind, for that matter." Mike Yarvitz, producer of MSNBC's *Scarborough Country,* took a more playful approach. In an on-air experiment, he drank enough tequila to replicate Gibson's blood-alcohol level. He then blogged, "Not feeling any anti-Semitic urges coming on, but that may be because I am Jewish."

At a progress hearing nearly a year later, Judge Lawrence Mira applauded Gibson for adhering to the terms of his probation. By early October 2009, the judge agreed to expunge Gibson's conviction. Gibson continued on from this debacle, though not from scandal.

On February 2, 2010, Gibson was interviewed by Chicago reporter Dean Richards via satellite. At the time, he was promoting his film *Edge of Darkness,* but Richards wanted the actor to revisit the DUI episode. Responding that the incident happened four years before, Gibson could barely hide his annoyance. With the rebuff, a chill set in and the interview soon ended. But before the microphones were turned off, Gibson muttered, "a-hole."

That interview moment played repeatedly online and on entertainment shows, a true testament to the foreverness of words—whether the speaker claims them or not.

Mastering Rule 16

Avoid the "do over" apology by getting it right in the first place. When you are in the wrong, come forward with a complete and sincere admission. Tepid acts of contrition suggest you are still not sure what, if anything, you did wrong.

Assume you have offended everybody. Do not qualify your apology with counterfeit phrases such as, "to anyone I may have offended ... " or "to those who took exception to my words ... " or "that's not who I am ... ." Apologies get silly when people try to distance themselves from something they are admitting.

Don't blame your actions on anything or anyone else. The diminished capacity apology is made of poor excuses, including alcohol and drug use, depression, fatigue, or a bad temper. Michael Richards of TV's *Seinfeld* sitcom blamed hecklers for provoking his anger, which then led to his yelling the "n-word" at the audience, repeatedly, when he was performing at a Los Angeles comedy club in 2006. While standing on stage, he gleefully recalled the pre–civil rights era when black Americans were often victims of hate crimes. Richard's unapologetic apology came via satellite on David Letterman's *Late Show*, with Jerry Seinfeld in attendance. He said he was "deeply, deeply sorry" for "flipping out." "I'm no racist. That's what's so insane about this," he offered, as if the angry words spoken that night belonged to someone else.

In 2010, when it was baseball player Mark McGuire's turn to apologize for using steroids, he portrayed himself as a victim of the times. McGuire issued a statement just after signing on as the batting coach for the St. Louis Cardinals. Of his ten year on-again-off-again use of steroids, he said, "It was foolish and it was a mistake. I truly apologize. Looking back, I wish I had never played during the steroid era." His apology was panned by sports fans.

Don't turn your apology into a confession. Mel Gibson said the right things in his second apology. The problem began with his interview, when he started responding to questions with excuses. Between pointing his finger toward the Middle East and confessions of pent-up resentments, he walked all over his apology.

Remember, an apology must be a leveling experience to be accepted. When Tiger Woods decided it was time to address reports of his marital infidelities in November 2009, he posted a message on his website. Ahead of more allegations, he posted a new message, this time mentioning "transgressions" he regretted with all his heart. On December 11, he released another statement on his site, still keeping his distance. Yet the media clamored for more. Then on February 19, Woods held a highly scripted event attended by staff, family, and supporters. Many were moved; still others noted that until Woods was willing to give up "control" his apology wasn't complete. Finally on April 5, five months later, Woods held a news conference and opened himself to questions. At last, he had stepped off his pedestal and could put the apology behind him.

Language specialists at the *Oxford English Dictionary* recently added an entry for the "non-apology," described as "a statement that takes the form of an apology but does not constitute an acknowledgement of responsibility or regret for what has caused offense or upset." They followed that up with the "apology tour," defined as "a series of public appearances by a well-known figure to express regret over a wrongdoing."

Avoid the "mock apology" unless you really don't care. With this scenario, the party has committed a wrong, but rather than offer up the real thing, they are defiant. Former Morgan Stanley analyst and Internet "It Girl" Mary Meeker was featured in a 2001 *Fortune* magazine article with the spoiler title "Where Mary Meeker Went Wrong. She may be the greatest dealmaker around. The problem is, she's supposed to be an analyst." Ms. Meeker wouldn't admit she was cheerleading stocks that she was being paid to evaluate. When she was ready to acknowledge the problem, it came off this way: Meeker interviewing Meeker.

MEEKER: *Do you judge Ted Williams on one bad year?*
MEEKER: *Did we do some deals we shouldn't have done?*
MEEKER: *Yes.*
MEEKER: *Did we recommend some stocks we shouldn't have?*
MEEKER: *Yes.*
MEEKER: *But, it's difficult to get hit and hit and hit when we did a better job than any other firm.*

Tactic
What to do when you are tired of talking about the thing you are being asked about? You "bridge" away to a different point

or message. Bridging is an important technique whereby you respond briefly to a question, then move the conversation from A to B. This is a useful device when dealing with repetitive, inappropriate, or unfair questions. The skill is in the use of a transitional phrase, a natural segue, so it doesn't appear as if you are dodging or ignoring the question. In bridging, use phrases like "the important aspect for the audience to consider ..." or "going forward, the ..." and then bridge to a message point. The media training technique "bridging" away is the opposite of "flagging," which draws attention.

Game Face Conduct

Sometimes it's better to decline an interview altogether. You are not obliged to put yourself in the hot seat if it's not in your interest to do so. Gibson's second apology had been accepted and he was fulfilling his legal obligations. The actor could not defend the indefensible and he gained nothing by trying. And in telling his story of the perceived unfair treatment, he appeared to be justifying his bad behavior.

And Finally

Do not overcorrect the problem. On December 5, 2002, Republican Senate Majority Leader Trent Lott offered a tribute at the 100th birthday celebration for Senator Strom Thurmond. He boasted, "When Strom Thurmond ran for president, we voted for him. We're proud of it. And if the rest of the country had followed our lead, we wouldn't have had all these problems over all the years, either." As many recalled, Thurmond had run for president on a segregationist platform. Lott's spectacular blunder ("the forty words" as he called them in his memoir) caused a fire storm of criticism

Not-So-Real Apologies

I would never want to demean him as an individual. I do apologize if he's offended by that. That was no way the point.
—Senator George Allen, on calling a cameraman of Indian descent, who was working for his opponent, "macaca" then adding "welcome to America," *Washington Post*, August 15, 2006

Now people are telling me that they have seen Michael J. Fox in interviews, and he does appear the same way in the interviews as he does in this commercial. ... All right then, I stand corrected.
—Rush Limbaugh, after telling his radio audience that actor Michael J. Fox was exaggerating symptoms of his Parkinson's disease in a television ad supporting embryonic stem cell research, rushlimbaugh. com, October 23, 2006

Although my lawyers tell me that my failure to immediately report this information is not a crime, I know I have let you down and have also let myself down.
—Tonya Harding, on the kneecapping assault on skating rival Nancy Kerrigan, *Washington Post*, January 28, 1994

and negative publicity.

Lott blamed the mishap on "a poor choice of words" while denying that he had embraced the "discarded policies of the past." After saying he was sorry to "anyone who was offended," he kept finding more and more people to offend.

By the time Lott appeared on Black Entertainment Television, he was overcorrecting the problem. Many were surprised to hear Lott tell interviewer Ed Gordon that he supported affirmative action "across the board," even though his voting record showed otherwise. (In fact, Lott had voted against a national holiday for Martin Luther King, Jr., the extension of the Voting Rights Act in 1982, and the Civil Rights Act of 1990.) But as he explained it, "My actions, I think, don't reflect my voting record." Too many apologies later, Trent Lott was forced to resign as majority leader.

Resist Self-Labeling

Be careful what you say about yourself, even on your best days, as your words may linger or reappear. Linda Evangelista emerged as one of the fabulous faces of the eighties. The supermodel made her remark quite lightheartedly, never expecting that hers would become the last word on the decade of excess. It was the time when luxury went mass market, corporate raiders joined society, and inside traders preached the gospel of greed.

The Supermodel's Minimum Wage

We have this expression, Christy and I: We don't wake up for less than $10,000 a day.
—Linda Evangelista

Zeitgeist: "spirit of the age," from the German words for "time" and "spirit."

[Tom] Wolfe took the title *[The Bonfire of the Vanities]* from the Florentine practice of literally torching anything associated with luxury. The most famous burning took place in 1497, when followers of Girolamo Savonarola—a monk with firm beliefs in austerity who consistently railed against what he perceived as an immoral society—collected and publicly torched objects Savonarola deemed to be associated with sin.
—Adam Gabbatt, "Quango lingo: Bonfire of the Vanities, and Other Inanities," *Guardian*, October 15, 2010

Near the close of 1987 two events more than any other captured the zeitgeist of the decade. In November, Tom Wolfe's mammoth novel *The Bonfire of the Vanities* was published. It introduced millionaire bond trader Sherman McCoy, the self-labeled "Master of the Universe." In December, director Oliver Stone unleashed the ruthless corporate raider Gordon Gekko in his film *Wall Street*. The fast-talking Gekko fired off sound-bite gems like "What's worth doing is worth doing for money."

It was the decade of President Ronald Reagan and Prime Minister Margaret Thatcher. They privatized industries and deregulated financial markets. Money was democratized—new or old—the distinction hardly mattered anymore. Living large was no longer in bad taste. On television, prime time was dominated by dramas featuring the super-rich Ewings on *Dallas* and the Carringtons on *Dynasty*. As film director Oliver Stone said, "Money was the sex of the eighties." The era of mergers and acquisitions saw a shift in the marketing of glamour and beauty, linking them to status brands. One could have sex appeal by possessing things.

In fashion, there was "the trinity," an elite sorority of professional beauties who shot to fame in the mid-eighties.

Canadian Linda Evangelista, American Christy Turlington, and British Naomi Campbell were the faces of the decade. Photographer Stephen Meisel was at the epicenter of their world. It was his idea to use the trio in high-voltage fashion spreads, elevating them from models to megabrands with unprecedented earnings. The March 9, 1992, issue of *New York* magazine reported that Turlington would earn $800,000 in twelve weeks posing for Maybelline cosmetics. "We completely re-invented the whole money thing—we make a ridiculous amount of money," she admitted.

Fashion writers were so enamored, they revived the term *supermodel* from the black-and-white decade of the forties. Popular culture transformed the supermodels, which included Cindy Crawford and Tatiana Patitz, into superstars. The trinity in particular acted the part. When the "girls" weren't turning heads sauntering down catwalks, they were partying with celebrities and even appeared together in a music video.

When the models descended on urban hot spots, they enjoyed the treatment usually reserved for movie stars. It was fitting, for the trio had replaced Hollywood actors as the symbols of wealth and glamour. They fronted multimillion-dollar marketing campaigns raising consumerism to dizzying heights. The greatest chameleon of all was Evangelista. She was signed as the face of Charlie, Revlon's popular fragrance. Her appeal was her versatility. Evangelista had an ability to alter her look—constantly cutting and coloring her hair—making her a stylist's dream. Actors get Oscars, but Evangelista's trophies were sixty magazine covers in three years.

In the summer of 1990, *Vogue's* Jonathan Van Meter interviewed twenty-five-year-old Evangelista for the magazine.

On October 6, 1942, the *Chicago Tribune* ran a story by Judith Cass headlined, "'Super' Models Are Signed for Fashion Show."

I hate it when they call us girls. Most of us are not girly, and we don't run our careers like girls. When I walk away from this, I'll have the luxury of doing what I like.
—Cindy Crawford, "Marketing Beauty and the Bucks," *Time*, October 7, 1991

Evangelista moved to the topic of money and how the fashion game had changed, giving the top models the winning hand. It was at that moment when Evangelista remarked jokingly, "We have this expression, Christy and I: We don't wake up for less than $10,000 a day." The quote was picked up, repeated, rephrased, and at times regaled, becoming for years the most notorious statement to come out of a muse's mouth. Critics mocked her temerity and wondered if any of the supermodels were worth the fees they were paid.

By 1993, there were signs that the heady ride was nearing its end. Fashion had a sudden love affair with grunge—the anti-couture. As the decade passed, the triumvirate had to make way for younger, generic-looking models. Evangelista departed the scene in 1998, choosing life in St. Tropez. At the start of the millennium, the luxury brands turned back to Hollywood, signing stars like Angelina Jolie, Uma Thurman, and Nicole Kidman to sell everything from watches to perfume.

Eleven years after her comment, the model and the interviewer came together again at a Manhattan restaurant. The topic: Evangelista's return to modeling after a three-year hiatus. "I was not 100 percent Miss Polite and Flawless," she said about her past attitude. "Maybe I was full of myself then. You start feeling invincible, but reality set in, and I'm not like that anymore."

"She's Back!" shouted the September 2001 issue of *Vogue* magazine, which ran the Evangelista interview in an elaborate twenty-two page photo spread. It was a glossy reminder of why the thirty-six-year-old model had been a sensation in the first place. But "The Quote" was not forgotten. Evangelista could explain it, dismiss it, and even reject it, but the label stuck. Her quote, wrote Van Meter, was

Gianni Versace was the designer who pushed that concept the furthest— reportedly he would outbid the competition to ensure that he got all the biggest stars for the same show, in the process inflating their rates from $10,000 to $50,000 for a half-hour appearance.
—Bob Colacello, "A League of Their Own," *Vanity Fair*, September 2008

The era of the Professional Beauty, or P.B., grew in Britain in the 1880s whereby reproduced images of "Ladies of Quality" were presented in store-front windows along London's Fleet Street. ... Lillie Langtry was the most celebrated P.B. The American version was the Gibson Girl, popularized by Charles Dana Gibson in the 1890s and 1900s.
—Evangeline Holland, "The Professional Beauty," edwardianpromenade.com

"used against all supermodels far and wide—but especially Evangelista, until it drove the supermodel train right off the tracks."

"I feel like those words are going to be engraved on my tombstone," Evangelista told Van Meter. "It was brought up every single time I did an interview," she says wearily. "I apologized for it; I acknowledged it; I said it was true; I said it was a joke. Do I regret it? I used to regret. Not anymore. I don't regret anything anymore. Would I hope that I would never say something like that ever again? Yes. Am I capable of saying something like that again? I hope not."

In 2004, Naomi Campbell, who was still a top model, won a victory after a British court ruled that the *Daily Mirror* newspaper had violated her privacy by photographing her leaving a Narcotics Anonymous meeting. The paper was ordered to pay £3,500. The editor, Piers Morgan, ridiculed the paltry sum, saying, "[She] or one of her colleagues once said supermodels wouldn't get out of bed for less than $10,000. This isn't even enough for her to pull back the bed clothes."

In the end, Linda Evangelista's characterization of her work ethos was more distracting than disastrous. This is usually the case with self-labeling. Still, interview subjects are always surprised to learn that even after they have moved on, the words they once flaunted can't easily be discarded.

Money never sleeps.
—Gordon Gekko, *Wall Street*, 1987

Mastering Rule 17

Avoid self-labeling. If you don't want it said about you, don't say it about yourself. You may want to call yourself a "geek," a "nerd," or "anal," "hyper," and so on, but think about what you put out there.

Don't tell audiences who you're not. Tell them who you are. No one knows the origin of the word "bimbo," but for a time the word was synonymous with the name of a former church secretary, Jessica Hahn. She was the woman at the center of the Praise the Lord Club (PTL Club) sex and money scandal. In 1987, Hahn accused Jim Bakker and another preacher of rape and she admitted taking hush money before changing her mind and speaking out. She posed for *Playboy* magazine and offered these words, "This is supposed to be the year of the bimbos, right? So let's start with the fact that I am not a bimbo." These injuries are self-inflicted (same goes for, "I'm not a mental case" or "I'm not a wife beater"), as nobody asked the question.

Avoid using negative stereotyping to prop yourself up. Richard Nixon attended a press conference on November 17, 1973 hosted by the four hundred managing editors of the Associated Press. Joseph Ungaro asked the president about his tax returns for 1970 and 1971. The president gave a long elaborate answer, took another question, and returned to the tax question again. This time he ended with the five famous words: "I am not a crook." Nixon's unsolicited comment made headlines. Over time, it settled into presidential lore as the most famous example of self-labeling.

Remember, if you wrote it, you "said" it. Every day you are depositing words into a personal library that defines you. This includes emails, speeches, memos, tweets, blogs, posts, perhaps even your diary. Any misstatements can be mined like gold in perpetuity.

Avoid speaking of yourself in the third person. You may attract the wrong kind of attention from reporters and amateur psychologists. As well, many find this habit, known as illeism, annoying. According to experts, it's a symptom of a personality disorder. *Esquire* magazine posed the question to Elsa Ronningstam, the author of *Identifying and Understanding the Narcissistic Personality*. As she explained, "Referring to yourself in the third person creates distance between 'I' and 'he.' So if you have an exaggerated view of how great you are, you could be using this distance to make yourself even bigger."

Game Face Conduct

Self-labeling is almost always self-indulgent chatter, which should be avoided when going on the record. If the self-labeling is harmless self-promotion, the media will likely ignore you. On the other hand, if what you say can be used against you, it will stick long after you have outgrown the sentiment.

And Finally

Remember, you brand yourself with words as well as attitude. Sean Combs, a.k.a. "Diddy" or "P. Diddy" or "Puff Daddy" or

Meanwhile, the rise of celebrity culture relegated many models to anonymity. ... A decade ago, models graced 10 of the 12 covers of American *Vogue*. Last year, only one model made the cover, and that was Linda Evangelista— she of the famous $10,000-a-day quote.
—Kiri Blakeley, "The World's Top-Earning Models," *Forbes*, July 16, 2007

just "Puffy," told reporter Katherine Finkelstein of the *New York Times*, "I am definitely at fault of my own image," after he indulged in a bit of self-labeling that proved costly. His company, Bad Boy Worldwide Entertainment Group, had branding attitude. In addition to music labels, he built a financial empire with a clothing line, a restaurant chain, and fragrances. According to the latest *Forbes* magazine tally, Combs had a net worth of over $580 million, "making him one of the richest figures in hip-hop." Puff Daddy's media messages were a big part of that. He had promoted himself as rap's "bad boy" and a "crazy genius." Combs thought everyone knew that his self-labeling was marketing, but then it began to sink in that the media expected him to, well, *act badly*. That image was a liability when in 2001, following a shooting incident that took place in a Manhattan night club, he was charged with and went on trial for gun possession and bribery. Combs was acquitted of all charges. The next day the *New York Times* reported the story under the Sinatra-inspired headline, "Regrets, He's Had a Few, Especially about His Puffy Image."

A word is dead
When it is said,
Some say.
I say it just
Begins to live
That day.
—Emily Dickinson, *The Poems of Emily Dickinson*, edited by Ralph W. Franklin, Harvard University Press, 2005

Know When to Get Personal

It's difficult to know how much is too much when asked
for a personal opinion, or how much of your own story
to share in an interview. A bad answer proved costly for
presidential candidate Michael Dukakis during his final
debate with George H.W. Bush. Dukakis was asked whether
he would still oppose the death penalty if *his* wife Kitty
were raped and murdered. It was a shockingly personal
question. Bush had already dubbed him "the Iceman," and
the defining moment froze the perception of Dukakis as,
well, a very cold guy.

The Iceman

No, I don't ... and I think you know that I've opposed the death penalty during all of my life. I don't see any evidence that it's a deterrent and I think there are better and more effective ways to deal with violent crime.
—Michael Dukakis

Two thousand people filed into Pauley Pavilion at the University of California to watch the final debate between Vice President George H.W. Bush and Governor Michael Dukakis on the evening of October 13, 1988. Most were campaign contributors, staff, friends, family, and volunteers—essentially warring camps of Republicans and Democrats seated on opposite sides of the aisle.

Three weeks earlier, sixty-five million Americans watched the candidates' first televised encounter. Political pundits awarded Dukakis the win, but barely.

Troubling for the Republicans was the persistent media buzz over Bush's lack of verbal command. George Will, writing in the *Orlando Sentinel*, described the vice president's signature style as "sentences that reel drunkenly around a topic." In its special issue on the Republicans that year, *Time* magazine wrote, "Bush seems to suffer from a kind of oral dyslexia."

The media was already rhapsodizing over Ronald Reagan's presidency, treating his final days in office as the end of a golden era. "Reagan is still widely perceived as the

Presidential debates always put more importance on projecting character than on being right.
—James Fallows, "When George Meets John," *Atlantic*, July/August 2004

model of a strong President," said *Time*. Even though Bush was half of the winning ticket that secured two terms in the White House, a Bush victory was not assured. Questions lingered over his ability to exude strength. At issue was the so-called "wimp" factor. As well, many were questioning his selection of Senator Dan Quayle as his running mate.

Cool and cerebral, Dukakis was a serious challenger. His election to three four-year terms as governor of Massachusetts set records. By the time he delivered his acceptance speech at the Democratic National Convention in late July, a *New York Times*/CBS News poll gave Dukakis a seventeen-point lead. However, less than a month later Bush grabbed a six-point advantage in national polls after his nomination at the Republican National Convention.

Bush had a formidable team that included the notorious Lee Atwater as campaign manager, the "tactical genius" behind the character assassination of rivals. "He can live without a friend but not without an enemy," observed *Time* magazine. Also onboard was media consultant Roger Ailes, who was responsible for Bush's television ads. According to *Time*, "Although Ailes may be adept at going for the jugular, he is also taking aim at the heart."

For Dukakis, the race was on to tell his story before it was told for him. Bush's operatives set out to diminish the Democrat as a Massachusetts "liberal." Liberal was a label Dukakis at first embraced, then failed to define, and finally abandoned. Atwater and Ailes zeroed in on Dukakis's vocal opposition to capital punishment and to their delight they found something to work with. The pair were about to write the playbook on negative campaigning.

In 1987, the *Lawrence Eagle-Tribune* ran over two hundred news stories on the controversial issue of prison

Republican political strategist Lee Atwater is credited with popularizing the term "defining moment" in the context of American political campaigns.

The Pulitzer Prize is journalism's highest award for excellence. The publisher of the *New York World* and the St. Louis *Post-Dispatch*, Joseph Pulitzer (1847–1911), made a provision in his will for the creation of the prizes in journalism, letters, drama, and education.

"If I can make Willie Horton a household name," [Lee] Atwater is reported to have said after the session, "we'll win the election."
—Paul Taylor, *See How They Run: Electing the President in an Age of Mediaocracy*, 1990

Willie Horton was what the Bush people called a "wedge" issue. It was an issue that separated people ... a "hot button" issue, one that drives people to instant anger.
—Roger Simon, *Road Show: In America Anyone Can Become President, It's One of the Risks We Take*, 1990

furloughs in Massachusetts. The coverage earned the newspaper a Pulitzer Prize. A hot-button topic got hotter because the program could be linked directly to Dukakis. In his first term, Dukakis commuted the sentences of forty-four, first- and second-degree murderers. He also vetoed a bill aimed at banning furloughs for prisoners convicted of first-degree murder. In 1987, the program—which Dukakis didn't create, but which his veto extended—led to the weekend release of a convicted killer named Willie Horton. While out, Horton, an African-American, broke into a home where he robbed its owners, stabbed the man, and raped his fiancée.

The public outrage prompted Dukakis to end the program. No matter, Atwater saw opportunity in Horton. The lurid details of his crimes fueled two controversial ads. In September, a pro-Bush action committee aired a thirty-second spot featuring a mug shot of a menacing Horton. The attack ad implicated Dukakis, while stoking race-based fears. A week later, the Bush team launched a slightly tamer version called "Revolving Door." Nothing the Dukakis camp could say about a 13 percent decline in Massachusetts' crime under his watch could quell the public's horror over Horton.

Adding to the havoc in Dukakis's campaign, another negative impression took root—that Dukakis lacked warmth. Bush called his opponent "the Iceman," and the sentiment was growing. The *Los Angeles Times* reported that while Dukakis had built his campaign on the theme of competence, he would need to "make a more personal appeal" in order to win.

Two days before the final debate, journalist Bernard Shaw was asked to moderate. And he would ask each man the opening question. Shaw was one of CNN's original anchors and a war correspondent, well-known for asking the uncomfortable question. On the way to Washington National Airport for the flight to Los Angeles, Shaw picked up a book on the Constitution and paused at the section on the Twentieth Amendment. He knew what he was going to ask Bush.

Late into the night, just hours before the debate, Shaw was up chain smoking in his hotel room, still searching for a zinger for Dukakis when an idea came to him. Shaw would prove to be as devastating to Dukakis as Ailes and Atwater.

On October 13 at 9 p.m., the final presidential debate got started. A stern-sounding Shaw introduced the debate panel. Then Bush and Dukakis walked out on stage to cheers and applause. In the adjacent pressroom, reporters sat at long tables eyeing the bank of television monitors.

After brief introductions, Shaw turned to Dukakis.

SHAW: *Governor, if Kitty Dukakis were raped and murdered, would you favor an irrevocable death penalty for the killer?*

Inside the pressroom came gasps from reporters. "What did he say?" some murmured. Onstage, however, if the governor was shocked, he gave no hint.

DUKAKIS: *No, I don't, Bernard. And I think you know that I've opposed the death penalty during all of my life. I don't see any evidence that it's a deterrent and I think there are better and more effective ways to deal with violent crime. We've done so in my own state and it's one of the reasons why we have had the biggest drop in crime of any industrial state in America, why we have the lowest murder rate of any industrial state in America. But we have work to do in this nation. We have work to do to fight a real war, not a phony war, against drugs. And that's something I want to lead.*

The reporters sensed it
instantly. Even though the
90-minute debate was only
seconds old, they felt it was
already over for Dukakis.
He had not been warm: He
had not been likable. He had
not shown emotion. He had
merely shown principle.
—Roger Simon, *Road Show:
In America Anyone Can
Become President, It's One of
the Risks We Take*, 1990

Back in the pressroom, shock turned to disbelief over Dukakis's wonkish, unemotional response. "He's through," said one. "Get the hook," said another.

Bush gave a one-minute rebuttal, and then it was his turn.

SHAW: *Now to you, Vice President Bush. I quote to you this from Article III of the 20th amendment to the Constitution. Quote: "If at the time fixed for the beginning of the term of the President the President-elect shall have died, the Vice President elect shall become president," meaning, if you are elected and die before inauguration day ...*

BUSH: *Berrrrnie.*

The vice president's mock-surprise response drew chuckles from the audience. Shaw didn't miss a beat.

SHAW: *... automatically automatically, Dan Quayle would become the 41st President of the United States. What have you to say about that possibility?*

BUSH: *I'd have confidence in him. And I made a good selection. And I've never seen such a pounding, an unfair pounding, on a young senator in my entire life. And I've never seen a presidential campaign where the presidential nominee runs against my vice presidential nominee; never seen one before.*

For the sixty-seven million viewers and reporters, one moment stood out from all the rest. Steve Daley of the *Chicago Tribune* wrote, "In a matter of figurative television moments, CNN anchor Bernard Shaw raped and murdered Kitty Dukakis, then killed off George Bush before Inauguration Day." Tom Shales of the *Washington Post* reported, "Moderator Shaw certainly got the evening off to a morbid start." Shaw was criticized for asking such an "ugly" question. The *Chicago Tribune*'s Timothy McNulty quoted an "embarrassed" Kitty Dukakis as saying, "It was an outrageous question, it really was."

While many believed Shaw provided the low point in the debate, Dukakis's failure to give way to a recognizable emotion was the big political story. His campaign manager, Susan Estrich, had prepared the governor to show empathy for victims of violent crimes. That was ironic given Dukakis's own story. His older brother had been killed by a hit-and-run driver and his aging father, a physician, was beaten badly by an assailant during a robbery at his medical office. Dukakis had missed the opportunity to get personal with voters.

Estrich went into damage-control mode, explaining to reporters that Dukakis had been unwell and had missed the day's final rehearsal. These details no longer mattered. Bush was not the new Reagan. Americans had not fallen in love with him. Still, Dukakis did not stand in the way of Bush's victory on Election Day.

A decade later, PBS's Jim Lehrer asked Dukakis if he wished he had handled Shaw's question differently. Dukakis straddled his answer. "Yeah, I guess so. On the other hand, I've listened and watched myself respond to that, but I have to tell you and maybe I'm just still missing it or something. I didn't think it was that bad. You know. But maybe it was."

Dukakis's response suggested that he was still trying to work it out in his head, which of course was the problem. The now-famous question was damaging precisely because the candidate was unable to summon his inner, less-cerebral self to show voters the man who would be president.

I fretted that if he really hit that question out of the park, I would be accused of having asked a softball question.
—Bernard Shaw, "A Fond Farewell to Bernard Shaw," *Larry King Live,* CNN, March 8, 2001

His campaign manager, Susan Estrich, later reflected, "When he answered by talking policy, I knew we had lost the election."
—Stephen Ducat, *The Wimp Factor: Gender Gaps, Holy Wars, and the Politics of Anxious Masculinity,* 2004

Mastering Rule 18

Remember, communicating is connecting with people. In order to reach or influence others, you must be willing to share something of yourself. Dukakis squandered the opportunity to get personal with voters by showing both the public and private man. He was qualified to speak as a victim of crime, with loss a genuine part of his story.

Don't cling to intellectual arguments when the situation calls for emotional intelligence. Psychologists John D. Mayer and Peter Salovey wrote the book *Emotional Intelligence*. They define it as "the subset of social intelligence that involves the ability to monitor one's own and others' feelings and emotions, to discriminate among them and to use this information to guide one's thinking and actions." Dukakis missed the cue to present a caring husband. He stayed on message, leaving Kitty to her fate.

Don't assume that lies will be seen for what they are. The fact is, negative messages and spin can be effective. Lies are often more compelling and less complicated than the truth. When attacked, you must hit back, and quickly, with a strategy to counter and contain. In 2009, twenty years later, Dukakis was asked again about the Horton offensive. He told interviewer Michael Bendetson, "I made a deliberate decision that I was not going to respond to the Bush attack campaign. That choice was just a huge mistake. It is not a question of forgiving the other side; you have to assume that

The debate—and perhaps even Dukakis's chance to inspire a late-inning rally to win the election—may have been lost in those opening two minutes.
—Walter Shapiro, "Bush Scores a Warm Win," *Time*, October 24, 1988

To be fair, Bernard's question had to have been the most personal question a member of the press had ever posed to a candidate for national office, but Dukakis's dry, matter-of-fact response was devastating to his chances.
—William J. Bennett, *A Century Turns: New Hopes, New Fears*, 2010

they are going to do anything and everything to win. The question is are you ready? Do you have a strategy of dealing with the attack campaign?"

Remember, you own the rights to your personal story. On May 14, 2013, Angelina Jolie wrote an editorial for the *New York Times* explaining her decision to have a double mastectomy, to reduce her risk of breast cancer. The Oscar-winning actress lost her mother and aunt to the disease. Jolie carried the defective gene, BRCA1, and wanted to make other women aware of this medical option. Jolie made headlines around the world—on her terms.

Know when it's time to assert your right to privacy over the public's right to know. An example of a subject pushing back comes from the world of sports. In 2001, Ray Lewis was named the 35th Super Bowl's Most Valuable Player and the NFL Defensive Player of the Year. Twelve months before, Lewis was held on murder charges following a stabbing incident outside an Atlanta nightclub. The charges were dropped but Lewis, who admitted giving a misleading statement to police, was sentenced to one year probation and fined $250,000 by the NFL. After that, the star linebacker focused on winning games and staying out of the spotlight. But he couldn't lie low on Super Sunday after his team, the Baltimore Ravens, captured the championship. Now he was facing a gaggle of reporters demanding information about the ordeal. Lewis had already given an intimate, detailed account of that night and the aftermath to ESPN. He refused to delve into the matter again, and he told the reporters why. "I'm not here to justify anything that went on because that's a story in my book that's closed, regardless of whatever

BARRETT: What's the wittiest, cleverest way you've said I love you?
STOPPARD: First of all, I have no idea, and secondly, I have a personality defect that precludes me from answering questions about my own intimate life, if I've ever had one, and so forth.
—Tom Stoppard and Amy Barrett on his play "The Invention of Love," *New York Times Magazine,* May 20, 2001

questions come up. What I went through, you can't get me to think about it or talk about it," he declared.

Don't share your personal opinion just because you're asked. In July 2010, President Barack Obama was wrapping up a news conference on health care reform when he took one last question. Reporter Lynn Sweet asked about the arrest of Henry Louis Gates, Jr., a prominent African-American Harvard professor. Gates had misplaced his keys and forced open his front door just as police arrived to check on a possible burglary. Gates was cuffed and arrested by police officer James Crowley after the two argued. After stating that "Skip," as Obama called Gates, was his friend and that he didn't have the facts, Obama continued with, "I think it's fair to say, number one, any of us would be pretty angry; number two, that the Cambridge Police Department acted stupidly in arresting somebody when there was already proof that they were in their own home."

Criticism from law enforcement organizations was swift. The president, normally adroit on the subject of race, was accused of injecting himself into a local police matter. Obama admitted that he should have "calibrated" his words differently. The controversy officially ended with a "beer summit." The president and vice president hosted Gates and Crowley at the White House. Obama cast the incident as a teachable moment. And it was, no doubt, for him. The final word though goes to Gates. When asked for his post-drink impression of Crowley he joked, "When he's not arresting you, Sergeant Crowley is a really likable guy."

Game Face Conduct

Shaping and sharing personal details to project a public image can have unforeseen consequences, for example: the self-described ideal husband, supermom, or high-minded philanthropist gone wrong. Obviously, any contradictions between your private life and public pronouncements can and will be held against you. Those who engage in myth-making can hardly complain after the fact that their privacy has been invaded. Like entries in a resume, representations made on the record invite investigation.

And Finally

Knowing when to get personal, or whether to get personal at all, is the question. Once you engage the media in your story, you do not get to disengage, no matter who you are.

From their wedding in 1981, Prince Charles and Princess Diana reigned over the global village. Media interest intensified after the fairy-tale marriage ended in separation and then divorce. But there was no precedent for the war the royals waged against each other in public. They began sharing secrets with reporters, turning newsrooms into private battlegrounds.

In June 1992, Andrew Morton's book *Diana, Her True Story* told of her suicide attempts and bulimia, and named Camilla Parker Bowles as the other woman. The book created sympathy for Diana. Charles began his charm offensive in 1994 with an ITN documentary called "Charles: The Private Man, The Public Role." It was a glowing portrait, but it was his confession of adultery that dominated the headlines. That caused more shockwaves for royal watchers, though the savviest of the set sensed that the prince was signaling his readiness to move on.

The oxymoron "global village" was coined by Marshall McLuhan. It describes the collapse of time and distance in the electronic age that allows us to share world events with the immediacy and intimacy of local villagers.

In 1995, Diana sat down with the BBC's Martin Bashir for a brash and calculated rebuttal, during which she confirmed that she too had been unfaithful. It was ironic. Both Charles and Diana gave interviews to enhance their images. What they did instead was devalue their currencies. If only they had taken their cue from someone who had been there. Getting personal with the press was one mistake American first lady Jackie Kennedy Onassis never made.

Onassis was an unassuming master of the game. One week after President John Kennedy's assassination, in November 1963, Mrs. Kennedy requested an interview with political journalist Theodore H. White. She urged White to write of her husband's one thousand days in office as the "brief shining moment" from the musical *Camelot* he so loved. The story that gave birth to the myth appeared in *Life* magazine. Over the next few months, she gave audio-taped interviews to authors Arthur Schlesinger and William Manchester. In the decades that followed her unpopular marriage to Aristotle Onassis, she was pursued, photographed, and hounded for interviews, but she never added her voice to the record. With every interview she didn't give, her currency appreciated.

HAINES: Why is America obsessed with Jackie O.?
VIDAL: We saw her picture for decades and she never talked.
HAINES: Why is America obsessed with Princess Diana?
VIDAL: We saw her picture for close to 20 years and she never stopped talking.
—Gore Vidal and Chris Haines, "The Salon Interview: Gore Vidal," Salon.com, January 14, 1998

Be Consistent, Be Yourself

Ellen DeGeneres tells the story with a smile. Before
acceptance and popularity came the hard decision to
speak openly about her sexual orientation. Her advisers
ruled against it. Ellen stayed the course, embarking on a
new career and racking up Emmy awards and blue-chip
endorsements along the way. The television host knew
what was false and what was real. Above all, she knew
herself.

The Master Class

When I made the decision to come out, everything was great.
And I really naively thought nobody's going to care, you know.
It's like, I'm going to just now say, by the way, I'm gay.
—Ellen DeGeneres

It's the Monday after Halloween, the kids are in school, and a grown-up party is underway at stage 2 of the Warner Brothers lot in Burbank, California. It's another fun day on *The Ellen DeGeneres Show*. The audience members are on their feet clapping and dancing to the music. Stained glass doors part, and in a state of excitement, some forget their dance moves. All eyes turn to DeGeneres, who is swaying and waving her arms. The New Orleans native is sporting her trademark tennis shoes and slacks.

DeGeneres is executive producer of the popular daytime talk show that premiered September 8, 2003. From day one, *The Ellen DeGeneres Show* drew praise from reviewers. "Knowing the strength of her comedy is grounded in silly, good-natured, apolitical banter, she has single-handedly set out to make daytime fun again. Critics are applauding the effort and viewers are taking notice," wrote Rhoshale Littlejohn of the *Los Angeles Times*.

DeGeneres rose to fame by commandeering a scenic view of the ordinary and taking audiences along for the

The privilege of a lifetime is to become who you truly are.
—C.G. Jung

ride. How to get the pumpkin seeds out of her niece's home-made Halloween costume or a tutorial on the Mexican holiday Cinco de Mayo, all reflected a singular style from her years of stand-up comedy. Back then, her stammering patter, topped by a deadpan earnestness, drew comparisons to entertainer Bob Newhart. After her debut on *The Tonight Show* in 1986, DeGeneres made history when she became the first female comedian Johnny Carson waved over to have a chat.

In December 2003, a profile in the *New York Times* praising DeGeneres was a reminder that she was a woman in recovery. "Ms. DeGeneres' life and career had looked like a train wreck for the last five or six years," reported Anita Gates. The bruising assessment was in reference to the comedian's decision to come out as a gay woman three years into her sitcom, *Ellen*, which aired on ABC.

In April 1997, the news officially broke in a *Time* magazine exclusive headlined "Yep, I'm Gay." A smiling, but secretly petrified, DeGeneres graced the cover. Inside, the comedian told of her uncertainty over the character's coming out. The real-life Ellen had taken a big gamble. "She has more at stake than ABC—which has watched this former top-10 show drop to No. 30 in the last two years—and Disney, which has already sold the reruns into syndication. There isn't exactly a big call for lesbian leading ladies in Hollywood," wrote *Newsweek* in its April 14 edition.

When her character, Ellen Morgan, came out in a one-hour episode of *Ellen*, it attracted a record-breaking forty-two million viewers. However, after back-to-back episodes about Ellen Morgan's lesbian life, the public grew weary and viewership fell. A deeper drop in ratings, amid criticism that *Ellen* had become "too gay," prompted ABC to cancel

Q: What made you a star?
CARSON: "I started out in a gaseous state, and then I cooled."
—Johnny Carson, responding to an audience member, *The Tonight Show Starring Johnny Carson*, NBC, 1968

That revelation could have ended her career, as she had to be aware, but she also knew she had to be honest. Thank God for Ellen DeGeneres.
—Bob Newhart, "Ellen DeGeneres," *Time*, April 30, 2006

the show a year later. The network's president, Robert Iger, told *Primetime Live* on May 6, 1998, "I think the audience left primarily because of sameness, not gayness."

Two years later, there was more heartache. DeGeneres's break-up from her girlfriend, actress Anne Heche, made tabloid news. In a September 2001 interview with the *Advocate*, DeGeneres described how the loss had leveled her. "I didn't leave my house. I would go through days of crying. It felt like I would never live again. But you do." That same year, CBS launched a sitcom, *The Ellen Show,* starring DeGeneres as a career woman who was gay. After only eighteen episodes, the network closed production due to poor ratings.

DeGeneres spoke to *People* in 2003 about coping with rejection. "I've learned that there's room for people to not like me," she explained. But people did like her. DeGeneres had recently been the voice of Dory, a dim-witted fish with an exasperating short-term memory, in the animated Walt Disney Company-Pixar production *Finding Nemo*. The film was a box-office hit and audiences raved about her work. In the same year, DeGeneres wrote her second book, *The Funny Thing Is.*

On November 8, 2004, DeGeneres joined Stone Phillips of *Dateline NBC* to discuss what was being called her "comeback." Her choice of confidant was interesting. Phillips was a news anchor best known for his investigative reports and crime stories.

PHILLIPS: *You exude so much positive energy on the show. Where does that come from?*
DEGENERES: *The liquor. I'm sure of it.*

Comedy is much more difficult than tragedy—and a much better training. ... It's much easier to make people cry than to make them laugh.
—Vivien Leigh, *Actors Talking About Acting*, John E. Booth and Lewis Funke, 1961

Phillips was curious about DeGeneres's effect on her celebrity guests, noting how many of them happily followed her lead with the quirky antics.

DEGENERES: *I'll do anything for a laugh. I love the show. I love doing it. I get so much from it. It's an amazing thing that I lost everything from being me and then I'm now just being me and it feels good on many, many levels.*

PHILLIPS: *You know, they say in life and especially in entertainment, there are no second acts. So, how did you do it? What do you think enabled you to make maybe one of the biggest comebacks in recent memory?*

DEGENERES: *I don't know. And I just kept coming back. I wouldn't stay down, you know. I could've. My feelings were really hurt. I was really sensitive. So part of it is luck and part of it is talent. And part of it is perseverance.*

PHILLIPS: *Was there a time when you wondered if your career in Hollywood was over?*

DEGENERES: *Oh, I didn't just wonder. I was sure it was over. Yeah, I was sure.*

PHILLIPS: *You were really at the height of your career at that point.*

DEGENERES: *Yeah.*

PHILLIPS: *And it really came crashing down.*

DEGENERES: *Yeah. When I made the decision to come out, everything was great. And I really naively thought nobody's going to care, you know. It's like, I'm going to just now say, by the way, I'm gay. I mean, all of my business people, all my people, were saying, don't do it, you know.*

Authentic: true to one's own personality, spirit, or character.
—*Merriam-Webster's Collegiate Dictionary,* 11th Edition

DeGeneres was making a statement about who she was; in the end that statement proved confining. She was indeed a pioneer, and a gay role model, but there was much more. The comedian had the recipe for lifting the heaviness of everyday life and infecting audiences with her gift for play.

DeGeneres was finally free of labels and ready for her best role. "With her daytime talk show, which is, essentially, a sitcom without borders, she has finally found herself squarely at home," wrote Joyce Millman in the *New York Times* in 2004.

The Ellen DeGeneres Show won acclaim and dozens of Emmy awards. Eventually, DeGeneres's brand of authenticity would appeal to big business. In 2005, American Express approached her to appear in its ad "My Life, My Card." On September 16, 2008, the fifty-year-old DeGeneres made an announcement on the show. "I am here to set the record straight right now. I am not pregnant. It just turned out to be a bump. I went to have it checked out," she quipped over laughter. The real news? "I am the new face of CoverGirl." She had signed on to promote the cosmetic label's "Simply Ageless" line. It was "a coup" and evidence that DeGeneres "has punched every ticket to mainstream success," noted the *New York Times*.

In September 2011, Ellen DeGeneres got the *Good Housekeeping* seal of approval by way of a cover story. It reported DeGeneres, "The former T.G.I. Friday's waitress from Metairie, LA, remains relatable even with a shelf full of Emmy Awards and a list of credits that include her sitcom, movies, hosting the Oscars, and writing best-selling books."

Anything could happen on *The Ellen DeGeneres Show,* where guests strut their stuff anytime—even seasoned newsmen and politicians.

Everybody, it seems, is inclined to dance to DeGeneres's tune once they come onto the set. When the show is over,

To be nobody-but-yourself—in a world which is doing its best, night and day, to make you everybody else—means to fight the hardest battle which any human being can fight; and never stop fighting.
—E.E. Cummings, "A Poet's Advice to Students," *E.E. Cummings: A Miscellany,* edited by George James Firmage, 1958

That's a tough balancing act [hosting the Oscars], but DeGeneres has mastered it. The key is that she both exudes and creates goodwill.
—Robert Bianco, "On balance, DeGeneres walked a fine, funny line," *USA Today,* March 3, 2014

DeGeneres cues the music for her ritualistic dance into the audience. They are back on their feet as she boogies, down and across the aisles, stops to dip, turn, and snap her fingers. DeGeneres is on top of the world, doing her best to take everyone with her.

Mastering Rule 19

Be yourself, your best self. Don't affect a different you for interviews. Audiences respond to authenticity above all else. Media strategist Michael Deaver tells a story that underscores the importance of being genuine and helps to explain why President Ronald Reagan was called "The Great Communicator." When Reagan was governor of California, Deaver asked his boss to indulge in a small contrivance to snag a "chance" photo opportunity. Deaver provides the details of their conversation:

DEAVER: *Mr. Governor, I have a great idea. I want you to take your jacket off and sling it over your shoulder and then we're going to walk out into the park in the state capitol and the feeling I want is pensiveness.*
REAGAN: *Mike, I can't do that.*
DEAVER: *Why not? It's very Kennedy-esque.*
REAGAN: *Yeah, but I'm not Kennedy. And let me just tell you that if I'm uncomfortable doing it, people are going to be uncomfortable watching it. So don't ask me to do something I can't do.*
—*A Different Drummer: My Thirty Years with Ronald Reagan,* Michael Deaver, 2001

Be Consistent. It's a lot easier to be consistent when you don't have to remember who you're supposed to be. Somewhere in the archives of Paul Krassner's satirical magazine *The Realist* (1959–2001) is a 1961 interview with

Playboy founder Hugh Hefner. Here's what the publishing pioneer said then: "A magazine is as young and as vigorous as the thinking that goes into it, and I hope to still be very much of a young man—psychologically, at least—when I'm sixty. Maybe physically, too. Charlie Chaplin fathered a child when he was seventy. And I'll have all those 'Playmates of the Month' around to keep my interest up." Hefner was thirty-four.

—Hugh Hefner with Paul Krassner, *The Realist*, 1961

Never let others define you. Take a lesson from a master. Henry Luce was the founder of *Time* (with Brit Hadden in 1923), *Fortune* (1930), and *Life* (1936) magazines. *Time*, a weekly digest of news for busy people, would revolutionize the magazine industry. *Fortune* would glamorize the business of making money, and *Life* would become the photo album of the American experience. It was Luce who coined the phrase "The American Century." For the decades following World War II, Luce was said to be one of the most powerful men in America. But Luce knew enough about the media and the true nature of power to resist the label.

REPORTER: *Do you think you have too much power for one man?*

LUCE: *It seems to me that's a very abstract question.*

REPORTER: *No, I think it's a very practical question.*

LUCE: *How can you measure power? You can't weigh it.*

REPORTER: *You surely have great power, do you not?*

LUCE: *Well, I wouldn't even say power.*

REPORTER: *You wouldn't say this is power?*

LUCE: *Influence and utter responsibility. I associate power more clearly and semantically with public office.*

Do not fear to be eccentric in opinion, for every opinion now accepted was once eccentric.
—Bertrand Russell

The way to develop self-confidence is to do the thing you fear and get a record of successful experiences behind you.
—William Jennings Bryan

REPORTER: *Yes, but your magazines certainly influence public office.*

LUCE: *Well, if you like the word.*

—*Henry Luce: His Time, Life And Fortune,* John Kobler, 1968

Not every interview is a matter of life or death. Give yourself permission to throw out talking points that sound canned—and have some fun! Actor Ian McKellen shows how it's done:

BARRETT: *Is playing characters who do horrible things more interesting than playing those who are good?*

MCKELLEN: *Oh, good characters are very difficult to play.*

BARRETT: *Really? More difficult than evil ones?*

MCKELLEN: *Oh, yes. I mean, do you know any good people?*

BARRETT: *I think I know a couple.*

MCKELLEN: *Yes, a couple, and don't you wonder at them and think, Goodness gracious me, what is their motive to behaving like that? It's so difficult.*

—Ian McKellen with Amy Barrett, *New York Times Magazine,* November 25, 2001

SWANSON: Yet you're a brand.

STARCK: Yes, but people don't buy me to show they have money. They buy me because they understand the intelligence. We shall invent the elegance of intelligence. And the beauty of happiness. Or the beauty of tenderness. I'm sorry I'm so pretentious this morning.

—Philippe Starck with Carl Swanson, "Tribal Chieftain," *New York Magazine,* May 2005

Showing vulnerability in an interview is fine. Assuming the interview is about you. DeGeneres was honest in expressing her pain, which is not the same thing as weakness. No one would ever accuse Muhammad Ali [formerly Cassius Clay] of being soft. Here is the twenty-two-year-old boxer opening up to *Playboy* magazine, eight months after he became the World Heavyweight Champion.

PLAYBOY: *There was another controversy about the honesty of your failure to pass the three Army preinduction qualification tests that you took shortly after the fight. Any comment?*
CLAY: *The truth don't hurt nobody. The fact is I never was too bright in school. I just barely graduated. I had a D-minus average. I ain't ashamed of it, though. I mean, how much do school principals make a month? But when I looked at a lot of the questions they had on them Army tests, I just didn't know the answers. I didn't even know how to start after finding the answers. That's all. So I didn't pass. It was the Army's decision that they didn't want me to go in the service. They're the boss. I don't want to say no whole lot about it.*
PLAYBOY: *Was it embarrassing to be declared mentally unfit?*
CLAY: *I have said I am the greatest. Ain't nobody ever heard me say I was the smartest.*
—Muhammad Ali with Alex Haley, *Playboy,* October 1964

Game Face Conduct

Stay true to yourself regardless. Interviewers are invariably looking for conflict or controversy. Still, it's a fact that more problems are caused by inner conflicts than by the questions posed. Take counsel from Nathaniel Hawthorne, whose nineteenth-century novel *The Scarlet Letter* explores the theme of authenticity. Hawthorne tells us: "No man, for any considerable period, can wear one face to himself and another to the multitude, without finally getting bewildered as to which may be true."

And Finally

We've met a lot of accomplished people for whom the defining moment proved embarrassing or too revealing. We've seen what happens when people ignore the rules of conduct for giving interviews. Under pressure and unprepared, many allowed their true selves to disappear, hidden from view behind fearful facades or arrogant poses.

Interviews are contests of skill. As with any ability, the art of giving interviews will come more easily to some than others. There is no magic involved—it's a matter of mastering the rules. Use the confidence you've gained to stay present, while summoning your best self to guide you. Now, you're showing your game face.

Mastery: knowledge and skill that allows you to do, use, or understand something very well.
—*Merriam-Webster's Collegiate Dictionary,* 11th Edition

ACKNOWLEDGMENTS

It is impossible to imagine the journey without Saada Branker, my researcher, continuity editor and guardian angel.

My heartfelt gratitude to talented advertising men and women: Ron Telpner, Bob Froese, Casper Jones and Dorothy McMillan, who provided all manner of material and emotional support.

I also wish to thank Norm Oulster, Magda Bogin, Peter McCluskey, Joe Suskin, Ronaele Rose and literary agent Sam Hiyate for their generosity and wise counsel.

Other friends of *Game Face* inspired the penny-dropping moments that helped shape my vision of the book. The honor roll includes Don Bastian, James McAvoy, Tommy Schnurmacher, Connie Wishner, Yves Sorokobi, Nicco Mele and Peter Himler.

Going back in time, I am grateful to the band of television news producers and editors who were my teachers and tormentors, and to our boss, Bill Cunningham, who turned me into an interviewer and, unwittingly, an author.

INDEX